TALES OUT OF SCHOOL

MEMORIES OF SCHOOL DAYS FROM BALSALL HEATH AND BEYOND

Edited by Val Hart and members of
Balsall Heath Local History Society

BREWIN BOOKS

First published by
Brewin Books Ltd, 56 Alcester Road,
Studley, Warwickshire B80 7LG in 2009
www.brewinbooks.com

ISBN: 978-1-85858-446-1

A Cataloguing in Publication Record
for this title is available from the British Library.

Typeset in Baskerville
Printed in Great Britain by
Cromwell Press Group.

Tales Out Of
SCHOOL

Memories Of School Days From
Balsall Heath And Beyond

By the same author:

Balsall Heath – A History, Brewin Books, 1992

Contents

Acknowledgements

This book is the product of many people who have contributed time, energy and expertise: recording and collecting memories, transcribing them, editing and proof reading.

Jim Fitzpatrick
Bron & Pete Salway
Anne & Alan Hemming
Chris Sutton
Diane Stead
Pat and Albert Johnson
Dr Lynne Bevan
Ally Sultana
Margaret Pendry
Reginald Brown

Our thanks are specially due to all those who have shared their memories with us. They make remarkable reading and constitute a significant bank of resource material for the future.

A mother's visit to school. 1909.

Foreword

Memory is a strange thing. We may not be able to remember why we have just come upstairs or where we left our keys or whether we turned off the cooker, but we can all remember our schooldays, whether they were spent in Ghana or Pakistan, Adams Hill or Balsall Heath. They may not, in every case, be the best days of our lives, but they will usually be the most vivid. But if you have left some of those memories in a drawer to gather dust, I guarantee this book will bring them back, as fresh as ever.

Let me share with you a couple of mine.

At my junior school in Wolverhampton (Elston Hall, if you want the name), we had a boy in the class called Michael, and he had one eye. I never did find out what happened to the other one, or perhaps I really didn't want to know. Michael was never the most attentive of pupils, if you'll excuse the pun, and if he got bored in class he would take out his glass eye and roll it idly about on the desk. Sometimes he would play a game of desk golf, flicking his eye in the direction of the inkwell and trying to score a hole-in-one.

If you were sitting anywhere near this it was not easy to concentrate on English lessons. The teacher was well aware of Michael's disruptive influence, and had trained a girl, something of a teacher's pet, to keep an eye on Michael, if you'll excuse this expression as well. So, just as the exciting 'last hole of the British Open' was about to be played, she would cry: 'Sir, Michael's playing with his eye again!' Back would go the offending optic and normality would return.

It's curious what you remember, isn't it? At secondary school – Wolverhampton Boys' Grammar – I recall that we had a particularly odd Maths teacher we nicknamed 'Creep'. There was something creepy and understated about him, but occasionally he would explode. Most likely we had failed miserably to get the hang of a quadratic equation, or were swapping football cards at the back of the room.

So he would beat the whole class. All 30 or so of us queued up at his desk, the line stretching around the room and he would clobber each boy in turn with a battered old slipper he kept for the purpose. If this was not surreal enough, there were even a few foolhardy lads who rejoined the queue and came up for a second or a third whack. Their logic, impeccable in a way, was that the longer they could keep Mr Noel engaged in corporal punishment, the less time there was left for algebra. Nothing, they reckoned, not even a bruised backside, was more painful than algebra.

My thanks to all the contributors to this book, whose stories and memories brought my own flooding back. It makes me realise, though we come from all four corners of this round earth, that we all have a shared past.

Dr Chris Upton
Newman University College, Birmingham

Introduction

Memories of days at school are special. They were a large part of our lives as we grew from childhood to maturity and from dependence to independence so they have a certain universality. However, there the common features stop, as clearly our experiences of school are infinite in variety.

The memories in this book span a century and were collected and recorded from 120 different people mainly connected to Balsall Heath in some way. Some of the older memories recall times when the strict discipline of the Board Schools held sway or describe the challenges of schooldays during the Second World War. More recent memories reflect the changes in our education system, the banning of corporal punishment and the raising of the school leaving age.

This book presents a far wider picture, however. Balsall Heath and Birmingham are now home to many people who have moved here from abroad and these school memories provide extraordinary contrasts between schooling in England and various other countries; America, Africa, Australia, Hungary, India, Ireland, Pakistan, Scotland and Wales. Schools from various parts of England as a whole are also widely represented.

Undoubtedly the move from one school to another was difficult for a lot of children but especially so for those who moved from one country to another as well. These memories offer some unique and fascinating insights into that experience.

Memory is fallible. The Society cannot guarantee the accuracy of what other people remember. However, it is the personal nature of these memories that make them important as they throw valuable light on emotions, attitudes and relationships which the written records can never provide. The memories have their own validity.

Val Hart

Chapter 1

Starting Out

First day at school was, for many people, distinctly memorable. One has to feel sorry for the children who really just did not want to go but even sorrier for the generations of teachers who had to deal with everything from crying and escapees to kicks on the shins. There is a smaller band of people who remember the event with pleasure and who were eager to embark on the new experience.

The children who faced the most difficult times, however, were those who moved schools and sometimes, not just schools, but countries too. Some of this was occasioned by the evacuation of schoolchildren during the Second World War, some by families moving home and some was the result of emigration and immigration. Such experiences were made more painful by prejudice and racism among staff as well as pupils. These were not the happiest times of some children's lives!

FIRST DAYS AT SCHOOL

So Many Pegs.
Bygate Infants School, Whitley Bay,
Northumberland, late 1950's.
The cloakroom was a worry. I remember all those metal pegs and not knowing which one was mine. I think I cried, as my mother brought a little piece of string the next day and tied it round my peg! The rows of identical pegs stretch endlessly when you are only five and small.
Wendy Beynon (née Forsyth)

We Are The Ovaltinies.
I went to a nursery school in Cheshire. We used to have a little hook with our face flannel and our towel. We all had a toothbrush and they taught us how to clean our teeth. Each day we also had a cup of cocoa or Ovaltine.
Gwen White

Pegs in the cloakroom.

I'm Not Writing On That!
On my first day in the classroom, I remember being adamant that the chalkboards were trays for dinner. I really thought they were trays.
Pam Mullin

Slates.
In those early days at school we wrote on slate. I think we wrote with slate too, and the school day was long; longer I'm sure than it is in the present day of 2008.
Joyce Ashworth

Day School.
Clifton Road Infants, 1950's.
In the days leading up to starting school, my mother was always saying to me, "You'll be going to school, you'll be going to school one day". So much so I thought that I only had to go to school for one day! I struggled a bit to go for the second day.
John William Brown

Escaping From St. Clements Juniors.
Nechells, c1966.
I remember holding on to a bar in the cloakroom with mom and another person trying to drag me off it. They made the mistake of sitting me close to the classroom door and I made a break for it. Learning from that mistake they put me at a desk furthest from the door and with another pupil primed to shout "Miss" every time I attempted to escape.
Mark Houldcroft

Me And My Dummy Started At Clifton Road.
I remember my first few days. I used to take my dummy to school with me and have a quick suck under the tables. I couldn't be parted from my dummy.
Victoria Jeffs

First Day, Exciting Lies.
1970's.
In the very first class at Perry Beeches we were all asked, "Who has a pet at home?" Most of the class put their hand up, including me. "Who has a dog?" I put my hand up. "Who has a cat?" I put my hand up. "Who has a goldfish?" I put my hand up, every time. I didn't really have any of them – or any other pet!
Peter Cole

Boys With Girls.
Meadows Primary. 1960's
Getting used to school was a question of getting into the rituals; getting the equipment around you, like your pump bag and the desk where we sat with our partner, boy with boy, girl with girl. It was only later in juniors that it was changed to girl / boy, but that wasn't late enough – in age – for us boys to be happy about it. We didn't want anything to do with girls in the juniors.
Chris Sutton

Learning To Play.
Clifton Road.
I remember the first year in the Infants with the sand pit, the play house, plasticine, the water sink; it was all great fun. Then came the learning, which wasn't much fun, but you don't realise how much you value it in later life.
Pamela Douglas (née Blenkiron)

Clifton Infants' School, Balsall Heath, Birmingham. This building is now part of St. Paul's School.

New Pupil, New School.
Langley Avenue School, Northumberland.
My first primary school was brand new. Everything was new – and whenever I hear the hymn "Morning has broken", immediately I am back in the Hall and in the first assembly that morning, standing in the second row from the front. There was a big stage with the most beautiful curtains I had ever seen, dark blue velvet. And the floor was pale wood, all shiny and new. We were given Songs of Praise hymn-books, pale blue, and stiff to open, and smelling of new books. The desks were new and square with lift up lids and chairs with grey metal legs and bendy wood seats. We sat in rows all facing the front.
Wendy Beynon (née Forsyth)

First Day Little Terror.
My older brother remembers my first day introduction to school because of the rumpus I made. He remembers my sandwiches, which were wrapped in newspaper, being projected sky-wards from a skirmish that I was having with a teacher. He still sees them in his mind's eye spinning upwards through the air. Worst of all, I remember lying on the floor between chairs and half under desks resisting attempts at getting me out, and my taking hold of a pencil then using it as a weapon and stabbing a teacher in the palm of her hand.
Michael Henry Fitzpatrick

The Tindal Street Kicker.
I don't think I could have been very happy with the prospect of school because my mother often reminded me over the years that I introduced myself by kicking the teacher across the shins.
Alan Hemming

Shocking First Day.
Adams Hill, Bartley Green, 1970s.
It was a horrendous shock. First day I walked into the school it reminded me of that programme "Please Sir" where they had all the adults playing the kids. That's what the kids in year four and year five looked like to me; grown-ups in school uniforms.
Kerry Smith

Tindal Street School, Balsall Heath, Birmingham.

New Experiences.

At my first school there were only about twelve people in a class and that was it, so that was quite small. My teachers were my first meeting with people who were outside of my family. Apart from them and the neighbours, doctors, people at the clinic – they were the first people I came into contact with.

Iram Weir

Cry Days.

Budapest, 1980's.

On the first day in school, Vizafogo primary in the district of Angyalfold, it was terrible; we couldn't hear what the teachers were saying because all of us kids were crying. This new environment was so different to what we were used to. At six years of age, for many of us it was the first real taste of school discipline.

Laura Szendy

Happy To Start.

I was quite different from the other children because I could hear all the kids crying and screaming and everything but I just left my parents and started playing with the water.

Sheikh Amina Khanum

Testing Times.

Aga Khan Foundation, Pakistan.

When you started nursery you had to take a test and the test was how you play with the toys to see if you can play properly. And then could you recognise any of the alphabet? This was for what we called kindergarten which you call nursery over here.

Naseem Somani

Bicycle Business.

Ghana 1970's and 80's.

I remember that first day very well when I went to school on a bicycle accompanied by my dad. The bicycle came in very handy during the following years, as I found I could hire it out to my fellow students for riding around the school buildings at lunch time.

Peter Owusu

Early days at Jakeman Road Nursery, Balsall Heath, Birmingham. 2000.

Smethwick Hall Girls Secondary.
1967.
What a difference the change of school made to my life, I was really happy to go to secondary school; for a start both my older sisters were there. I remember the school was so welcoming and friendly. I loved writing with a nib and later got my first fountain pen, I really liked to write with it, and I still use one today when I want to write a nice letter.
Marcia Vizor

Nervous.
When I moved on to secondary school I was nervous and didn't know what to expect. I didn't want to leave my old friends and my old school.
Sameera Bi

SCHOOL UNIFORM

Daily Mail Clothing.
Uniform was optional at Clifton Road because most families could not afford it. Poor children had "Daily Mail" clothing – jerseys, boots and shoes. These were clearly marked so their parents couldn't take them to the pawnshop to get money for them. I always wore a dark dress and a white pinafore for school.
Mrs Osborne

Clothes Do Not Make The Man.
In the juniors the school motto "Clothes Do Not Make The Man" was painted high up on the end wall of the assembly hall in a semi-circular plate, rather like the name of a steam engine. The words became a very meaningful sentence to me. I have never been overawed by smartly dressed authority although I now recognise that the objective was probably to offer those of us who came from poor homes some palliative for our patchy appearance. It has to be kept in mind that this happened in the period 1926–1931. Those were the days of "Mail Fund" boots and stockings provided at Digbeth Hall.
Ted Wright

Raggy Trousers.
In 1930 we had a school cap with a badge on. Most people were poor, no-one could afford school uniform. A number of the boys wore ragged trousers with the seat hanging out.
Bernard Jackson

The Full Rig-Out.
The school did not have an official uniform and keeping us kids clothed was always difficult for our parents. We often went to the Post and Mail building at Digbeth where families could get clothes and free boots for the children. I remember getting a full rig-out, including socks, pants, and a dress.
Gladys Ford (née Woolley)

All White.
I spent all of my schooldays at Clifton Road School. Three of us sisters attended there and we were known as the Bickerstaffs with the whitest pinafores.
Annie Farrington (née Bickerstaff)

Getting Our Uniform.
My first school memory was having my first pair of long trousers. My brother and me had to dig up the headmaster's garden so that he could buy us our first pair of trousers for the school.
Jim Atkinson

Somewhere Handy.
Cheshire 1920's.
You had a pocket in your knickers to put your handkerchief in.
Gwen White

Clean and white pinafores for May Day. Early Twentieth Century.

Accidents Will Happen.
Dudley Road Council School.
My gran was a seamstress and I was supposed to have a pair of navy blue knickers. Well, we couldn't afford them at the time, so my gran made me a pair out of an old butcher's apron. Anyway I got to school and put my hand up, because somebody said you had to put your hand up to go the toilet. Well the teacher wouldn't let me go so I just stood there in the middle of the class...... luckily I had got my wellies on. She said to me, "I think you ought to go home". I said, "Well if I go home my gran will smack me and I suppose I've got a smack off you". She said, "No you're very lucky we've got some spare pants here", and she washed my wellies out.
Maureen Smith

Tieless.
Mico Practising School Jamaica, c1962–65.
My earliest memories of my schooling in Jamaica are of a regime of discipline. This was apparent for instance in the strictness surrounding the wearing of school uniform. It consisted of a navy blue skirt, a white blouse and blue tie, with white pumps. The white pumps were to be laced properly and kept gleaming clean. Every morning and evening rows of shiny white pumps would catch the eye as we marched up and down corridors on our way to and from assembly.

One morning we were running late for school and when we got there the head master was waiting for us. It was at this point I realised that I wasn't wearing a tie, and so did the head master. I received a stroke of the cane on each hand for my trouble. I was eight years old.
Marcia Vizor

Picking The Roses.
Wakefield High School for Girls.
Here was an establishment with pretensions of being a public school. It was a half way house – 50% of its pupils paid fees, 50% were awarded scholarships. The wearing of a school uniform was supposed to be a leveller. The school bucked this idea by seeing that the uniform was expensive and exclusive. It could only be bought from one very posh shop. It consisted of a white square necked blouse and a light blue and navy blue pinafore dress. A summer variant was a light blue dress or "shirtwaister". As a girl my mother had won a scholarship to Wakefield and was very proud to wear the uniform. Her grandmother, a seamstress, made her a blouse with an embroidered rose on the collar, something totally contrary to regulations. She got into a lot of trouble with her family for unpicking that rose.
Joyce Ashworth

Not Dressed For Comfort.
Wallesey High School, mid 1950's.
I was sent to the High School; complete with new leather satchel and regulation brown lace-ups. Oh, we felt smart in our navy pinafore dresses, white shirts and striped ties. Hats were worn, with a badge and elastic under our chins; but woe betide those who were seen without this headgear on their way to school. They had to wear those hats all the next day, and everyone knew they'd been caught.

For gymnastics we had green linen tunics, with square necklines and reaching exactly to the knee when kneeling down. Knickers were to match, also in green linen, and not the most comfortable of fabrics for underwear! Adolescent girls would refuse such garments today!
Wendy Beynon (née Forsyth)

Those Blazer Pockets.
We wore square necked tunics with a square necked blouse underneath in winter, with cotton dresses and blazers in summer. I remember the blazer pockets always had nasty stained patches in the pocket corners where soggy bits of things collected. Navy blue berets were worn – or rather thrown about.
Anita Halliday

Hand Made Clothes.
Grove Park Grammar School for Girls, Wrexham.
In winter we wore the usual uniform of the time – navy blue gymslip, white blouse with the school tie. Outdoor wear was a navy blue gabardine or school blazer with the school badge sewn onto the breast pocket and what were called, I think, riding hats. These were made of felt and had a turned up brim, turned down at the front, with a ribbon in the school colours around the crown. These were sometimes customized by altering the shape of the brim by pressing it up flat against the sides. If you were caught out of school not wearing any part of the uniform it meant certain detention. In summer I think we had boaters. The summer uniform was a cotton frock printed in the school colours of red and blue on a white background. No off the peg

Summer and winter uniforms at Grove Park Grammar School, Wrexham. 1950's, including Bron Salway (née Jones).

ready made items, the material had to be bought from Lloyd Williams, a local ladieswear and haberdashery shop and then hand made. At the boys' school, a separate school and building, built tantalizingly across the road, I remember that they wore short trousers and peaked caps. Imagine that today.
Bron Salway (née Jones)

Begging Hat.
Smethwick Hall Girls Secondary, 1967.
The school had a strict rule – you weren't allowed to get on the bus for a trip without a beret. I forgot mine on one occasion and had to go all around the school begging people to loan me a beret and of course it needed to fit over my big hair.
Marcia Vizor

Too Green.
My uniform was green at primary school and then bottle green again for another seven years at secondary school. I shall never wear green again!
Sheikh Amina Khanam

Country Schooling.
Thermopolis High, Wyoming.
At the age of 14 years I moved up to High-School, Thermopolis High, which was a mixed sex school. There wasn't a school uniform, but there was a dress code for girls. A white blouse was to be worn with a dark skirt. Minimum make-up with the wearing of modest jewellery was allowed. This was to contain any fashion competition and protect both the girls and their parents from expense.
Ron Vannelli

It Makes A Change.
I really liked my uniform. I was the first person in my family to wear a proper uniform as my older sister wore the traditional South Asian dress and my mum was very pleased to buy me a uniform. It was a white shirt and black or blue trousers.
Sayma Bibi

White Shirts Weekend.
Ghana, Africa, 1970's and 80's.
Our secondary school, where we sat O levels, was the Sunyani boarding school, Broig Ahato region. Our uniform comprised a blue shirt and blue trousers with red shoes. At weekends we changed to white shirts with khaki shorts, we thought we were really cool.
Peter Owusu

The Fit-All School Uniform.
Nairobi Kenya in the 1980's and 90's.
There was a strict regime about the wearing of school uniform; it consisted of long socks, and long baggy shorts. The socks had to reach the knee and usually met up with the shorts. These were teamed with an over-sized shirt with short sleeves, that is except for Fridays when we wore long-sleeves. If we didn't have a uniform for a legitimate reason, we had to dress smartly or we could expect to be caned.
Rizwan Janmohamed

Uniform.
When I came over from Pakistan my mum used to put lots of Indian clothes on me or dress me up in ridiculous army outfits or things that she thought were quite modern but were modern in Pakistan. So when I came and found everyone wearing flares I used to get quite embarrassed, so eventually I persuaded my mum I needed to have the same clothes as everyone else, and I started to wear nice little dresses and shoes.
Iram Weir (born in Pakistan and educated in England)

You'll Grow Into It.
I remember that my parents bought me a uniform that was a little too big so that it would last me, but a lot of families couldn't afford uniforms so we wore more or less what we wanted.
Abdullah Rehman

Marked By Your Clothes.
Jaffray Academy, Mombasa, Kenya, 1980's.
We wore an olive colour Kota, white trousers and a white scarf. If you didn't wear the right uniform points were taken off from your annual exams. So if you got an "A" but all the year round you had worn the wrong shoes you could be marked down to a "C".
Sukaina Khimji

ON THE MOVE

Reduced Circumstances.
I was six when I first entered the portals of 'Clifton College' having attended Tindal Street School during the previous year. Upon the death of my father we had moved from the affluence of Edgbaston Road, (where everyone kept at least one maid-servant) and had taken up occupation of 18, Hertford Street, which my mother

thought would be more in keeping with our reduced circumstances. Alas, even then she was over optimistic for eventually we were forced to flit from there, owing rent!

I was a shy little girl with long fair ringlets, but as I did not easily make friends and spoke rather differently from the other children, my parents were Londoners, I was quite mistakenly regarded as being 'stuck up'. Only Mr Wright seemed to like me, and in return I liked, then loved, then positively adored him. He was young, handsome and he lauded my work: oh, if only he would remain single until I was old enough to marry him!

Valerie Harris (née Farrant)

Travelling To England.

I moved to England when I was nine, my great aunt and uncle; my mother came to the UK when I was four years old. It took us two weeks to travel to the UK by boat. I was very seasick. My memory of travelling from the village and going to the boat are sad ones as I didn't want to leave. I still remember how dark and vast the sea looked. I had to climb the ladder to get onto the big boat. I came to this country through the traumatic experience of coming on the ship and seeing my family that I didn't know.

I met my parents after a long time, also seeing my brothers and sisters. I had to fit into a new family; and fitting in a new family was difficult. My parents found a school for us, which was very different to the school I left behind in Grenada. It was very traumatic. I had to settle into junior school and then after a year move onto senior school. Everything was different, everyone spoke different and it was a different culture and different topics at school.

Yvette John

WWII Evacuee.

I was evacuated to Wales and found that Merthyr RC Infant's school buildings were like the majority everywhere; brick-built Victorian design. The playground had a stony dirt surface; no greenery, no tarmac, no nothing.

Back in Birmingham as the war ended, I was sent to St Thomas C of E at Bath Row. I was not happy there, in fact I hated it. I had lost the only friends I had known, and no one at my new school could understand my Welsh accent.

Pat Johnson (née Shine)

Outside Toilets.
St. George's Road Primary School, Wallasey.

At age 10 I moved south to Cheshire. St George's Road Primary was a red brick Victorian building with separate entrances for Boys and Girls, and playgrounds were separate too. The primitive toilets across the yard would be condemned as

Pat Johnson (née Shine) at St. Thomas C of E School, Ladywood. 1940's.

unsuitable today, but we thought nothing of crossing the big yard to reach them in cold, wet or snowy weather.
Wendy Beynon (née Forsyth)

Nineteenth Century Heating in the 1940's.
I moved to Moseley Church of England National School which dated from 1828. The heating in a number of classrooms was provided by open coal fires, fine if you were seated at the front, very chilly at the back – especially near the windows. The school did not have a school hall but two of the classrooms were divided by a floor to ceiling wooden concertina partition, which opened to provide an assembly area.
Alan Hemming

Coming From Pakistan.
I came from abroad and needed to be assessed so that the school could decide what groups they should place me and my twin sister in. We were both sat down in an empty hall to do our test and then sent home.

There was no such thing as separating for personal development reasons so we were put in the same classes for almost everything. It did help because we didn't start school at the beginning of term so friendships had already been established. It did help that we were together.
Shahida Aslam

Under Cover.
Kingston, 1960's.
Around the age of ten I found myself at a new school, I cannot remember why I went there or the school's name. I believe I have blocked it out of my mind deliberately as I had an awful time there. I do remember that the school building wasn't completely closed in. There were low walls and a huge roof with nothing in-between save for roof supports. All of the school classes gathered under this roof where we were divided into separate groups. Each group would then go outside with a teacher to begin lessons.
Marcia Vizor

Caribbean Emigration To The UK.
George Betts C. of E.
My parents had joined the exodus from Jamaica looking for work and a better life in England. At first, while they got established, we kids were left with foster parents at home in Kingston. Eventually we were sent for and I found myself in Handsworth attending George Betts C of E School. I was one of just two black children in the whole school. My thick Caribbean accent didn't help my assimilation and integration into school life. We were teased so much and the Americanisms I used, like 'Gas Station', 'Gasoline oil', and 'sidewalk', brought even more attention from the teasers.

My hair was long and thick and constantly being pulled by the other children to see if it would come off. I was called names that I had never heard before. I was being bullied and the teachers, with this happening right in front of them, didn't do anything to stop it.
Marcia Vizor

Marcia Vizor (née Daubon) after arriving in Birmingham from the Caribbean.

No Longer A Twin In School!
Bristol, 1960's.
At the age of eleven I went to Merrywood Grammar School for Girls, and for me the over-riding sentiment was "Wow, I'm away from my brother" I really did feel that. It was the constant comparisons being made between me and my twin that made me feel that way. My mother had a further set of twins after us and because of our experiences she demanded that our siblings be separated and taught in different classes.
Marion Ridsdill

School Down Under.
Brooklyn State School, Melbourne, Australia, 1950's.
I recall my early days at school in Melbourne, shortly after our arrival in Australia. We were living in an Immigrant Hostel in Brooklyn and the school playing fields backed on to it so it was only a quick sprint to get there in the mornings and home at night. I was one of a school full of immigrants from all over Europe and many couldn't speak English; there were, of course, some Australian children too from the nearby houses. The school itself was of wooden construction, painted in pale green and surrounded by huge gum trees. Morning assembly was always outside. When I drove past it years later, I remember thinking it looked a typical Australian scene, quite lovely really! There were only a few classrooms, because it was expected children wouldn't be there long once their parents got jobs and moved off the Hostel and into their own homes, so it was bit like a conveyor belt. We had Shelter Sheds away from the school perimeter, where we would eat our lunch and it was our shelter during play times if the weather was too hot or too wet.
Janet Jones (née Blewitt)

Moving Overseas.
We moved over to the United States and that was a big thing; the school there was completely different. That transition was horrible, I found it very difficult. I rarely spoke to anyone, friendships had already been forged and I felt like an outsider.
The vice principal took me to my first class and announced me as "Samantha from London, England" which of course I wasn't. The other students stared at me as though I was an alien. Every single morning in class, we had to pledge our allegiance to the flag of the USA, we put our hands on our hearts and facing the flag made the pledge. Thinking back, over the short time I was at junior high, I became depressed. I didn't make any friends there, and the work that they were doing I had already covered back in England.
Samantha Hines

High School.
The Bronx, New York, 1980's.
Things got better when I moved up to High-School despite being told by a fellow student that "Evander Child was the worst High School in New York". I was told that "You get beat-up if you're quiet, and beat-up if you're a trouble-maker". I thought, "I'm in trouble here".

I was thought of as posh by my American contemporaries because of my English accent. This had not helped my assimilation into school life at Junior High, but it did not seem to matter so much at the High School. I made a friend of a girl

whom might have been considered my opposite. Delilah had a Mohawk hairdo and wore punky clothes, and there I was, all prim and proper. We did connect and became great friends.
Samantha Hines

Along the Dirt Road.
Glendo, Wyoming.

I was brought up on a ranch in Wyoming; two of my pre-high schools were in small towns and a third in the countryside. The first of these three was Glendo School, Glendo Town. It was 12 – 15 miles from my family's ranch, along a dirt road. This road was impassable during winter, so we took a flat or apartment in Glendo in order to be able to attend school. My mother, who worked at the school as a cleaner, also rented an apartment during the 2 – 3 days prior to my starting at Glendo.

The school building was of brick, small and square, and untypical of other school buildings in Wyoming because of its flat roof. Most had slanted roofs with an apex. Four rooms in the building made for 12 classes. One teacher would look after three or four grades of an age group in each of these classes.
Ron Vannelli

Country Schooling.
Manderson, Wyoming.

My family rented land rather than owned it and this made it possible to move from farm to farm (or ranch). When we moved to Manderson, the change of school meant I now had a shorter journey, 3 to 4 miles, which could be taken by bus on a paved road. The iconic yellow school bus picked me up at the same spot, every school day. I remember that on my first sight of it, Manderson seemed gigantic in size compared to Glendo. Like Glendo it was built of brick which was notable at the time because schoolhouses were usually made of local wood. I believe that the Second World War had influenced this change.
Ron Vannelli

SCHOOLS OF EVERY VARIETY

At School In The Early Twentieth Century.

My school was on the Bristol Road when I started. We were a mixed group of boys and girls who were taught together until we were ten when they separated us. We were taught in a large room with beaded curtains and on the shelf above the door there was a stuffed swan. We started to learn from little cards, a fresh one each day.
Winifred Berkeley

Victorian Bricks.
Loxton Street Juniors, Nechells 1940's.
In retrospect, the knocking down of Loxton school building some years ago seems almost criminal. I remember it as a small Victorian red brick building. When entering you passed under a porch into the hall. The classrooms were off this, and at each end of the hall was a spiral staircase leading to further classrooms above. At playtime the duty teacher would blow a whistle and say "Everyone pick-up the litter nearest to you". In that way we would help keep the school clean.

It may sound old fashioned today but I believe the school sat in a working class, poor but honest district. It was surrounded by old tenement buildings and back to back houses with the communal toilets and courtyard.
Dennis Hammond

Corner Heating.
Cheshire 1920's.
There was a stove in the corner of each classroom for heating.
Gwen White

Cold Dark School.
I remember the heating radiators of the school were massive things, huge compared to me as I was only a titch. The radiators seemed to be everywhere but the school was still cold and dark.
Reginald Arthur Brown

Together Till Seven.
1930's.
I went to Clifton Road Infants School. The entrance was in Hertford Street and there were mixed classrooms of girls and boys until we went to the big school. At about seven years we were split up and the boys were taught downstairs and the girls were taught upstairs.
Jack Billington

The Thirty-Nine Steps.
Mary Street School. 1940's.
The classrooms at Mary Street School were furnished with wooden desks, joined in pairs, with the seat attached. The teacher had a high desk which had a cupboard underneath, and there always seemed to be a roll-front storage cupboard. Heating was provided by large pipes which ran around the edge of the room. The toilets were at the far side of the playground. The playground sloped slightly so in the winter

Belgrave School, Balsall Heath. This was originally Mary St School. After rebuilding it became Heath Mount School.

children used to make slides. This made getting across to the toilet quite a precarious journey. Once I slipped over and put my front tooth through my lower lip.

When we moved to the Juniors we moved across into the two-storey part of the building, which had two stone staircases, one at the front of the building, and one at the back, which led down to the playground. This staircase was always referred to as "The Thirty-Nine Steps".

Anne Hemming (née Davis)

Rural Location.
Ireland.
My school, Castlepollard Parochial School, County Westmeath, Ireland was set in a rural location in a small Irish town. The school was seven miles from my home and had only twenty two pupils aged from four to fourteen with one classroom for all such pupils. The teacher's house was situated at the front of the building where she resided. The school room had a cosy atmosphere with an open fire at one end and next to that the teacher's desk where she would sit facing the pupils.

Valerie Ganderton

Castlepollard Parochial School, County Westmeath, Ireland. 1950's.

Village School.

My family moved to Peasemore, a small Berkshire village, in 1944. I was eight years old, having moved from Birmingham. The village school had two rooms separated by a folding wooden screen. The main room for the older children, approximately 12 in number, had a large cylindrical coke fired stove. This provided heat for both rooms. Privileged children sat in the front desks near the heat. Others, like myself, sat at the back. The hole at the top of the stove, into which the coke was poured, had a circular metal cover with a moulded imprint of a tortoise. It was said among the older children that, when the tortoise became red hot, if you touched its tail it would run up the chimney!

We sat at wooden desks in pairs. Each of the desks had a lifting lid over a small storage compartment. The wooden seat and backrest were attached to the desk by wrought-iron bars. At the front of the desk was a shallow trough for pen and pencils and a hole into which was placed a white china inkwell filled each day from a large earthenware bottle of ink.

Peter Davis

Off Site.

Moseley C of E School 1940's.

The lack of facilities at the school for the practical subjects meant that for one afternoon a week the senior boys went to College Road and then Wheelers Lane

schools for woodwork and the girls to a house in Balsall Heath for domestic science. To travel to these schools we were given red and green plastic tokens to the value of ½d or 1d (halfpenny or one penny).
Alan Hemming

Silent Learning.
Wallasey High School, 1960's.
Classes were big and 32 of us sat in neat rows, at desks with lids and where we kept all our books. Coats were hung in the cloakroom each morning, and so we only had to carry the books needed for our next lesson or two – much less tiring than the heavy bags and clothes carted from room to room by pupils today. Lessons were predictably formal and silence rigidly enforced – if you chatted you were sent to stand outside on the balcony in full view of the Headmistress's study.
Wendy Beynon (née Forsyth)

A Bit Of Polish.
A rather strange memory from my days at school was that at the end of each term we had to bring in some furniture polish and a duster so we could polish our own desks, which were wooden, of course.
Val Hart (née Cooper)

Rubbish Store.
George Dixon, 1985.
We had the old desks with the inkwells still full of crusty old chewing gum, tissue paper or shavings. It was just vile.
James Hobbs

Hot Springs.
Thermopolis High, Wyoming.
The buildings were of two storeys, and brick built. There was an auditorium, a science lab and music rooms among others. The sport fields were vast and in constant use. Hot springs nearby provided for privately run swimming baths.
Ron Vannelli

Partition.
The main school building was a solid brick built affair, oblong in shape, with a single corridor running the length of the building. This was entered via steps from the playgrounds at each end. All the classrooms were off to one side of this corridor, and each classroom was separated from the next one by a large

permanently fixed partition which was pulled out from the side wall, along a groove in the floor. There were several of these partitions allowing for up to three or four classes, which when pushed back, turned the space into an assembly hall.
Michael Henry Fitzpatrick

It's What The Bike Shed Was For.
Essex and Lincolnshire, 1970's and 80's.
The bike-shed within the school itself provided cover for having a quick drag on a cigarette. We could expect a slap if we got caught.
Patsy Stewart

Self Contained.
Ghana, Africa, 1970's and 80's.
The school buildings and surroundings included an oil palm plantation which we used as a garden and a walking area. A ring fence completely enclosed us and we had to get an exit-form to be allowed past the security guard on the manned gate. The compound was very organized, it had places where we slept, classroom buildings for lessons, and an admin block where the headmaster had his office. One building doubled as the social meeting place and for church services. On Saturday nights it was filled with tables and chairs for a quiz and there was a small dance area for the Disco. The furniture was all cleared away for the church service on Sunday.
Peter Owusu

A Garden Of Our Own.
Chislehurst and Sidcup School dated from the 1930's. It had a big quadrangle with two storey buildings round the sides. It also had massive playing fields with a groundsman to look after it all. There was also a big herbaceous border and a Birthday Garden which was the special project of one of the art teachers. In October each year we celebrated the school birthday and were all asked to bring in bulbs to plant. Each form had a section of the garden and it had a pond in the middle.
Anita Halliday

Model Railway.
Mount Pleasant Secondary School.
The Mount Pleasant school buildings were rather old and in need of refurbishment even then. Whole classes had to be accommodated elsewhere and I found myself going to the Jenkins Street Institute for a term or so. It had lecture theatres, which

Mount Pleasant School, Balsall Heath, Birmingham. Joseph Chamberlain College opened in these buildings in 1983.

we used as classrooms and a big assembly hall with a gallery that was a favourite venue at playtime. The whole building became an adventure; we would sneak up to the projection room or trek downwards to the large cellar. One large room, being used for art had a partitioning wall which could be rotated on hinges to the horizontal, and on one surface was fixed a train set of scalextric proportions. The Art teacher was as enthusiastic as we boys were to play with it.
Mark Houldcroft

Like Colditz.
Kings Norton Grammar is housed in a huge solid brick Victorian building. With a war memorial in front of the main gates, the effect was of an imposing monolithic edifice. The staff in mortar boards and gowns were ready to go from the moment their pupils arrived, in a testosterone fuelled environment. I did a lot of reading during my years there and had read prisoner of war escape stories; often I found myself comparing KNG to Colditz. The place had an institutionalized feel; if you were remotely sensitive you did not want to be there.
Chris Sutton

CULTURE CLASH AND RACIAL DISCRIMINATION

Stereotypes.
Some of the teachers were nice, some of them were ok and some of them were a little bit unpleasant. I think they had their stereotypes of what an Asian girl should do when she was 16, and that was that she would get married. So I felt that they were giving their attention to those they thought were going to further education even if someone was misbehaving, which was frustrating.
Razia Khatun

Compulsory Urdu.
We didn't have much choice over subjects at school, we had to learn languages, and we had to learn French, which I didn't like very much. I didn't want to take Urdu as a GCSE either but I had to. All the Asian people were put into Urdu classes, that's the way it was then. I didn't like history because the teacher used to threaten to hit us with a ruler. It was that year the ruling came out that teachers were not allowed to hit pupils.
Sayma Bibi

Racism.
Some of the teachers were encouraging. But I did experience racism. There were two teachers in particular who were racist; it was obvious in the way they treated the black and Asian kids. I think in those days it may have been rife in some of the schools, but at the same time there were a lot of teachers who were very encouraging.
Yvette John

Black All Over.
I was told one time by my teacher that I was black but I would soon turn white because I was now in England and what would happen was the black freckles on my skin would reduce and get smaller so eventually I would become white. So I ran home and told my mum, who was horrified.

Also the same teacher asked us to draw a picture of what we did on our school holidays and of course everyone drew a beach. I'd never been to the beach but I drew one because everyone else was drawing one. I drew my family and myself in swimwear and the teacher asked me, "Are you black all over?" I said "Yes", and she said, "Isn't your tummy white and your back white?" She thought that because we were clothed away from the sun underneath we would be white. So I had to explain to her yes, we were black all over.
Pam Mullin

Fighting for my place in Birmingham.
Sandy Point Primary and Ladywood Follett School, 1960's.
My family brought me to England and Ladywood when I was just nine years old. My first experiences of an English school were of fighting, mostly because of the colour of my skin. I felt I had to prove myself to the other kids, that I was a person not just a colour. I did not find teachers at Ladywood Follett School very supportive during this time. I learned to ignore racial taunts and just get on with life.
Errol Thomas

United Kingdom?
Ysgol-Y-Gadr, Wales.
There was a lot of difficulty with racism because I was English and most of the people in the school were Welsh so often I used to get bullied because of that.
Stephen Gwynne

Watch out for the "Gippos".
My first school was Sidcup Hill and my attendance there was accompanied by dire warnings from my mother: "Gippos" came up to the school from the camp at Footscray and I had to be careful not to talk like them or mix with them in case I caught nits.
Anita Halliday

Heath Mount.
A multicultural school with little history, it was open to new ideas. Before attending Heathmount the only culture I was aware of was that of my Muslim family. The mix of pupils at school made for a lively environment in which to learn. Children of large Pakistani and West Indian communities served the school with their offspring. I remember particularly that a boy named Thomas was the only white pupil in the school.
Nazreen Bi

All In Together.
Camp Hill, 1990's.
Camp Hill was about 50% Asian and 50% white, with a small Afro-Caribbean group. Most of my friends were in fact white but there was good interaction. There wasn't any segregation.
Naveed Somani

Heath Mount School Choir entertain at a Victorian event at Highbury, Birmingham. 1990's.

Apartheid.
South Africa, 1960's.
For my secondary schooling I attended a public/private school in Pretoria which catered primarily for the children of Ambassadors. Their parents didn't feel that the South African state system was good enough in comparison with the rest of the world and so the school was based on the English system of education, with many English staff, including the Head Teacher. Here I discovered how little the state system offered in terms of world information and realised the meaning of the word censorship. The major advantage I had was access to the massive Embassy libraries and so I was able to read books that were banned and English newspapers which did not have articles blacked out and which weren't three or four weeks old.

The logic of the Government was that the less you knew what was happening in the rest of the world, the less you'd be able to say you'd been discriminated against or treated unfairly. Even worse, the Dutch Orthodox Bible was altered to prophesy that black people were created by God to be used as slaves.

There was no racism at the school which had diverse nationalities. It was open to black South African children but I remember only one such pupil attending, probably because it was fee paying. His father had made a lot of money running a liquor store in Soweto.
Shashi Bhana

DISABILITY

Harsh Help.
Victoria School, Northfield and Coventry 1970's and 1980's.
They thought at both my schools that people with a disability wouldn't get a job so they didn't really bother teaching us. I went to what they call a Special School but up to the age of eleven I was made to walk so I could be "normal".

I used to enjoy going horse riding and that helped me because it stopped me having to have a back operation. We also used to have physio and it was hell.
Ann Tolbutt – wheelchair user

Chapter 2

Inside The School Gates

The journey to school occupied a lot of people's minds. Walking to school was the order of the day for many children in various different countries and the distances covered by quite small children each day are staggering.

Memories of lessons varied. Some subjects such as History, Geography and Religious Education, were definitely not memorable whereas English, Maths, Science and more practical subjects evoked vivid recollections. Sport of all kinds featured strongly, with a rather pronounced bias towards memories from boys rather than girls. Almost nobody made positive comments on how much they had learnt.

Teachers, too, had a fairly mixed representation in people's memories. A few were recalled as inspiring but these memories were far outweighed by the echoing sense of unfair treatment and injustice.

THE SCHOOL DAY

Lining up in the playground ready to go into class at Clifton School, Balsall Heath, Birmingham. 1990's.

All Play and No Work.
Clifton Road, 1930's.
We had to be at school at 8.55am to line up and march into the classroom ready for 9am. The prefects took your name. If you were late twice you got the cane. I was late twice but the second time I nipped through the infants' playground and got in that way.

We had two hours playtime from 12pm–2pm. We played football for the first hour, 20–30 of us playing with a tennis ball, then we had to hurry home before father came home at 1pm. We all ate lunch together and then we had to be back in school for 1.55pm. We had two fifteen minute breaks in the morning and afternoon, the last one being at 3pm or 3.15pm and we finished school at 4.30pm.
Jack Billington

A School Day.
Somalia.
The climate was very hot so we used to start at 8.30 and finish at 1.30. From home to my primary school was one and a half hour's walk – each way. Every morning we started by saluting the Somali flag and singing the national anthem. Then we recited verses of the Koran and went to classes.
Abdulahi Ahmed

The Walk To School.
My church school in Wythall had two rooms. One was for the 5 to 7's and one for the 8 to 11's. I walked there from my home which was two miles away across the fields and up a lane. There weren't any school lunches for most of the time I was there so I went home to lunch and did that walk four times a day.
Betty Thornicroft

Break-Time And The National Sport.
Sandy Point Primary, St Kitts, West Indies c1960.
The school day started at 9am and finished at 2pm. That might seem like a short day, but this was natural for a hot country, making allowances for the heat of the day. These hours included breaks as well as a lunch period. We all lived close by the school and went home for lunch. The 40 minute breaks were more often than not taken up by the game of cricket; we

all wanted to play cricket from the age of three or four. That was until football came around, and then we all switched to football.

Errol Thomas

Pakistan.

We walked to school about two miles. We had a nanny and she used to take us and bring us back. It was a long walk and we weren't allowed to stop anywhere – it was straight there and straight back.

Naseem Somani

Good Afternoon.

Melbourne, Australia.

We had reading, spelling and sums in the mornings and drawing and stories in the afternoon. I remember most of us loved the afternoons best; the teacher would tell us to put our heads on the desk if we wanted to. It was always very, very hot – no air conditioning in those days.

Janet Jones (née Blewitt)

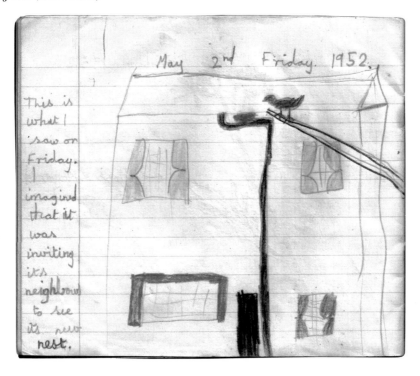

A bit of Nature Study from 1952.

CHALK AND TALK

The Clicker.
Clifton Road School.

I started at Clifton Road School when I was four and a half years old. There were about 30 children in a class, two to a desk. Education was free and the subjects taught were English, Arithmetic, History, Geography and Needlework. We went to Dennis Road School for Laundry and Cookery.

The teachers took all subjects and would stay in a class for twelve months. The hours were 9am – 12 noon and then 2pm – 4pm with two playtimes. The teacher would use a 'clicker' to get the attention of the class. This was a polished wood gadget which the teacher would press between finger and thumb. Writing was done with a pen made of wood with a steel nib. All books were supplied by the school. We didn't have library books. Sometimes we had drill in the playground. This was usually just arm exercises and marching.

Mrs Osborne

Lessons Make Money.

Our lessons covered the three R's plus one morning lesson on Religion by the Vicar. In addition we had one lesson a week of handicraft. This was a money making venture, as once a year the school had a sale. This raised money for a day out to the local town swimming pool.

Peter Davis

Changed History.
South Africa.

The whole state school curriculum was biased. History was their version of South African history not world history. Literature was also restricted to white South African writers. Shakespeare was not on offer.

Shashi Bhana

Just Routine.

I think school was too rigid for me, I felt I was doing the same thing over and over again, which can be quite frustrating but I think it could have been worse. The school that I went to helped me in some respects and we just have to make the most of what schooling we have.

Ishtiaq Khan

LEARNING TO READ, WRITE AND SPEAK THE ENGLISH LANGUAGE

Left Handed And Tied Up.
Clifton Road School.
Anyone who was left handed they tied their hand behind their back to make them use their right hand.
Rose Pearson

Not A Penny Difference. 1940's.
One teacher used to always hit the back of my hand with a ruler because I was left handed and it wasn't allowed. She just thought I was being awkward. It didn't make a penny difference. My work was so untidy when I wrote with my right hand that I used to change the pen over when she wasn't looking, but then if she caught me again she used to cane me.
Maureen Smith (née Roberts)

Turned Out Well.
There was one really good teacher I remember. I actually bumped into him some time ago and he was amazed that I was doing really well because when he knew me I couldn't speak a word of English and now I was a university student.
Dalal Olewa

Relearning the Language.
I learnt to speak English at school because apart from watching TV that was the only way I learnt to communicate with other children. I remember sitting at a desk in primary school and learning sounds of the letters because my mum had taught me a different kind of English to the English they spoke in England and I remember having to relearn it in a different way.
Iram Weir

Words In A Tin.
Meadows Primary School. 1970's.
I had a tin of words to learn my spellings. I remember aeroplane was the longest I had. The words were written out on card by Miss

Literacy Hour at Clifton Infants' School, Balsall Heath, Birmingham. 2000.

Guest using a black marker pen and then she would cut the words out and you took them home in your tin and learnt so many words a week. So you learnt how to read and spell from a tin of words.

I still have my first reading book, it was called "Here We Go – with Janet and John". It was like "Come Janet, come John, see the dog run", "Here is the red ball". It was very interesting stuff!
Steve Sutton

Too Good?
Clifton Road.
To further endear me to my classmates I excelled in sums, spelling and composition; indeed, one of my efforts concerning the adventures of an old hat was highly praised and read aloud to the whole class as an example of sheer perfection. Perhaps the small beginnings of a literary career? Yes, I can now quite see why it was I had no close friends!
Valerie Harris (née Farrant)

Self Taught.
Wyoming.
The family moved again and this time I found myself attending Lucerne Country School. From an academic point of view it became immediately apparent that I was not up to the standard of education that Lucerne pupils were, in fact they were way ahead of me. Early on the other kids gave me a hard time about this, especially when I couldn't read as well as them. I did catch up, partly due to the inadequacies of one teacher. She was getting on towards retirement and may not have been all that interested or simply tired. Whatever the reason, we kids played her up, giving her a hard time, perhaps a little too much of a hard time. She gave us little to do in the way of academic work, in fact almost nothing at all. I liked reading by then and compensated for the lack of work by reading more and more stuff, for instance I loved short stories, and there was time for me to read the entire Encyclopaedia Britannica while at school.
Ron Vannelli

Somalia.
It was very different. We didn't have problems or anti-social behaviour. Pupils were always respectful. I learnt Arabic, English and the Somali language.
Abdulahi Ahmed

NEEDLEWORK, SEWING AND KNITTING

Made To Keep.
Clifton Road, 1950's.
I still have, and use, a needle case that I had hand sewn in cross-stitch.
Yvonne Rollins (née Stead)

A Bit Of A Knit.
The art teacher was horrible, and I didn't like art at all. He gave me an ultimatum one day and told me that if I didn't do better work I would go into the knitting class. So I became the only boy in knitting class.
Jim Atkinson

Clifton Road Calamity.
Knitting lessons were another calamitous area so far as I was concerned. A lady teacher whose name I forget took the girls amongst Mr Wright's class for these, and they occurred with dreadful regularity upon Wednesday afternoons. No matter how I tried I just could not get the hang of it, and I received no help from home for my mother could not knit either. As my weekly time of trial approached I used to panic, for the use of the cane was permitted in those days. Even though I managed to escape it I was haunted by the possibility.
Valerie Harris (née Farrant)

Sewing Room at the Blue Coat School, Birmingham. Early twentieth century.

Sew Annoying.
Clifton Road.
When I was about 12 we had a Miss Ashmore who taught us to sew. I was already used to a sewing machine and seemed to spend my last 12 months at school cutting out and stitching flannel nightdresses. This intensely annoyed my mother. She said that she didn't send me to school to teach others to sew – I could be of more use at home. Therefore on my 14th birthday I left, much to the annoyance of Miss McKenzie who was left with several unfinished flannel night dresses!
Emily Jones (née Belcher)

The Dishcloth.
New Broughton Primary School, Wrexham, 1950's.
When I was at school we used to have knitting lessons and you started off by making a dishcloth.
Bron Salway (née Jones)

Unpick That.
The needlework teacher gave up on me and I read out loud to the rest of the class instead. She just could not go on saying every week, "I'm afraid you'll have to unpick that".
Anita Halliday

Shortie Nightdress.
I have still got a nightdress I made for my mother, a long nightdress – which is a tragic tale. I took it home and she didn't like long nightdresses and she cut it in half because she wanted a knee length one. I remember thinking "Oh my god, my beautiful nightdress ruined".
Kerry Smith

Domestic Goddess?
Conway Secondary Modern, 1950's.
We had to hand sew an apron and cap in the first term at Conway Road. The following term we had to wear these for Cookery Classes. I remember carrying a wicker basket with the ingredients needed to make whatever was to be taught that day. As our mothers had supplied the items for this lesson, we took what we had made home for the family. Not always very successfully.
Diane Stead

MUSIC

Play It Again, Pat.
Use of musical instruments was encouraged. For me this was mostly to be done at home as I played the piano.
Pat Johnson (née Shine)

Mouthwash.
Glebe Farm Park, Stechford.
Miss Waiklin, the music teacher, was in her 70's at the time, and pupils were wary of playing recorders in her class because she was so fastidious about cleanliness. You could always taste Dettol on the mouthpiece.
Ron & Gladys Ford (née Woolley)

Some Folk.
One of the senior mistresses at Moseley C of E School was a Mrs Bacon who lived directly opposite the school gates. She was elderly, very kind and firm, standing for no nonsense. She was keen on impressing upon us the need for speaking properly, being polite and conducting ourselves correctly. She loved music and tried to instil in us her fondness of English folk songs – "Greensleeves", "English Country Garden" and whenever I hear the rousing "Jerusalem" Mrs Bacon springs to mind.
Alan Hemming

SCIENCE

Stinks and Tears.
The worst, however, was chemistry where the teacher favoured the most boring approach possible. She read aloud from the textbook while the class took notes, except me. I was almost always standing outside in the corridor worrying about the head coming past. I still don't know what I did to be ejected so frequently, sometimes within a few minutes. The rest of the class found it extremely funny.

A Science Class studying salt, at Dennis Road School, Balsall Heath, Birmingham. 1891.

The French teacher was entirely different and I enjoyed her classes. She believed in huge doses of Gallic passion and energy, which involved exciting sessions with flying board rubbers and chalk, with the occasional burst into tears.
Anita Halliday

A Science Experiment.
We used to go to Sparkhill School for science until they built a new science block at Clifton in the last few years I was there, about 1931. Mr Lewis our science teacher taught us about electricity. There was a generator with 100's of volts. Mr Lewis told us to stand in a ring and touch it – which we did – and we all got a shock. If only one of us had touched it we would have been badly hurt.
Jack Billington

21st Century Science.
I find science technology interesting. I planned how to make an Olympic machine that could be used for the Olympics. If anyone was cheating they could find it out.
Zainab Bi

WOODWORK AND METALWORK

A Woodwork class for boys.

The Jekyll And Hyde Woodwork Teacher.
Highgate, 1970's.

The woodwork teacher was one we pupils loved to hate. In school he had a very stern and brisk manner, I think he was ex-army, and didn't appear to like kids at all. He would march around us as we worked at our benches uttering comments such as, "That's rubbish, scrap it and start again". He expected us to be at our benches, apron on, with our work and tools ready within ten minutes of the class starting. Ten minutes before the end of class time he would give orders to clear up, put tools away, sharpen chisels ready to start work again in the next lesson, sweep up the sawdust, hang up our aprons, and finishing with "Get out the lot of yah!".

Mark Houldcroft

A Metal Manual Class In The 1920's.

When the average age of the class was eleven years we were required to attend a metal manual class for one afternoon each week at the Manual Centre which stood in the grounds of Rea Street School. Mr Revell, the instructor, was a heavily built man of about fifty years of age. The first thing I remember seeing when we entered the works was an inscription high up on a wall. It was written in the Old English style of writing and said "Only the Best is Good Enough". We soon found out that this was a standard he expected from everyone. He instructed us in the correct way to hold tools and equipment and was always on hand to help and give advice when operations such as filing, soldering, drilling and forging had to be carried out. We made items including a fish slice, a name plate and a twisted poker. He would always compliment a lad on a job well done and would often reward us with one or two shillings from his own pocket. In later life I feel that many a lad would have been grateful to Mr Revell for the instruction he gave them.

Len Baron

P.E. DANCE, MUSIC AND MOVEMENT

Illuminating class.
Dudley Road Council School.

I used to do P.E. with the clubs. If you were going to do a display they used illuminated clubs. They would turn the lights out and when the clubs were going you saw the flashing lights going round, it was lovely.

Physical Education with Indian Clubs at Dennis Road School, Balsall Heath, Birmingham. 1891.

We used to do what they call pyramids where as many as six or seven people would make up a shape. I don't think they would do it today as sometimes you jumped as many as five high off shoulders.
Maureen Smith

How Sweet.
Uplands Secondary Modern, Smethwick 1954–1958.
I was terrified of heights but I was made to climb a rope in Gym. When I got to the top I would not come back down because I was frightened and just clung on. The teacher, Miss Hermley, shook the rope until I fell off.

I was the Captain of the Hockey Team and at the end of term, when I was leaving, we had to play a team of our teachers. Miss Hermley was the captain of the teachers' team. She must have played for all of five minutes, because when I bullied off I hit her shins and not the ball. Sweet revenge!
Marie Wilkinson (née Collins)

A Different Perspective.
Kings Heath Birmingham.
We had a Gym for PE with ladder-like bars up the walls. We seemed to be continuously hanging upside down from them. There was also a wooden-horse for us to vault over.
John Bealt

Physical Jerks.
Because the school did not have a hall our physical education took place in the playground, weather permitting, and consisted mainly of "physical jerks", stretching, running on the spot and ball games. Each week we walked from the school to Kings Heath Swimming Baths for swimming lessons. Fortunately these were the last period before lunch so those not taking school meals were able to go straight home, via a visit to Woolworth's on Kings Heath High Street, and not have the return walk to school.
Alan Hemming

Butterflies.
We had Music and Movement at school with a radio programme. I always remember the woman, a very posh woman, saying, "Go, find a space everyone, find a space, and wave your arms like a butterfly" or "Right, everyone pretend you are an elephant".
Jo Lea

Folk Dancing at Dennis Road School, Balsall Heath, Birmingham. 1936.

Trees.

We did mime and dance exercises in the hall. In one I had to pretend I was a tree. Someone played piano or whatever and you had to grow using your hands and stretching, shooting up, being a tree.

Steve Sutton

Ballroom Lessons.

Deykin Avenue School, Witton, 1940's.

Our school had mixed classes, which was very unusual in those days, so we had ballroom dancing and tennis lessons.

Ron Wilkinson

MATHS AND COMPUTERS

Class of 45.

Mental arithmetic tests were done every day on thin strips of paper just wide enough for your answers, and you were allowed to use pencil. Classes were huge by today's standards – I remember 45 in mine.

Wendy Beynon (née Forsyth)

Thirteen Times…

Maths at school was learning tables, which were ingrained into you by chanting. I left school at 14 and got a job at the Post Office. Someone asked me how much 13 times 12 was and I hadn't got a clue. All the tables finished at 12 times 12.

Graham Pearson

Parrot Fashion.
At my village school in Wythall we sat in rows and learnt our tables parrot fashion, right up to the 15 times table.
Betty Thornicroft

Knuckle Down.
Miss Hill, my teacher, was very strict. She was tall and strong and taught arithmetic. She was determined to make us understand her lessons and used the pointer on our knuckles.
Winifred Berkeley

From Little Acorns.
Colmer's Farm.
In 1979 Miss Reece, a Maths teacher, started a computer class as part of an after school club. They only had one computer for the whole school, that was it, and they only had spaces for thirty children. I put my name down and I remember there were about 200 interested and I didn't get into it as my Maths was not up to scratch. Of course now you don't need to be great at Maths to use a computer. It was a BBC Acorn computer. I was very disappointed.
Steve Sutton

PLAYING THE GAME

Going Swimmingly.
Head Taller.
I never learnt to swim but because I was tall I used to be a helper to the shorter children. My head was always above the water so I was useful. I don't know why I never learnt, I think they thought if I fell in I would be alright anyway.
Victoria Jeffs

A Way To Learn.
Handsworth, 1970's.
The school took us for swimming lessons to a Baths near Handsworth Park. It was an old Victorian building in Laurel Road, probably Grove Lane. We went on a regular basis without making much progress, – we messed about a bit. When a new instructor arrived, she watched us for a time and told a few of us "It's about time you lot were able to swim". She put me in a harness which was like a dog lead on a pole and took me to the deep end. I went under several

times swallowing water. I nearly drowned and the experience put me off swimming for life.
Samantha Hines

All For Fashion.
Rushcliffe Secondary, Nottingham.
In the swimming pool I did become a reasonable swimmer though at one time I almost drowned on the altar of fashion. I had really thick hair extensions woven into my own hair; they were the length of my back. It was too much to push in a swimming cap, so I tied it up in a bobble. In the water I found that I couldn't move as fast as everyone else. I was slow and heavy and it was down to my extensions getting wet. I realised I was slowly drowning with the weight of my wet hair.
Selina Brown

Sporting Passions; The Loved And Hated.
Smethwick Hall Girls Secondary, 1967.
When it came to sport I loved running and hated swimming. This for me was firstly simply inconvenient because of my hair. Being long and thick I had a terrible time getting it inside a swimming cap. If my hair did get wet mum would have to wash it and it took a long time to dry. Anyway swim caps were so unfashionable, being decorated with flowers. Secondly was my reluctance to get in the water at all because I didn't like water on my face. A teacher helped by pushing me in to the pool. I had to sink or swim. I sank.
Marcia Vizor

The Best Baths?
Loxton Street Juniors, 1950's.
Loxton Street School had little onsite facilities for sport so we had to travel. Woodcock Street Baths provided for swimming and field sports were played at Stechford. The baths for the time were state of the art, complete with high diving boards. A bus took us to these places.
Dennis Hammond

Those Australian Swimmers.
My family moved home when my father, a teacher, was transferred. My new primary was South Bunbury. Sport was a big part of the school curriculum. I took up swimming, and featured in school swimming carnivals. This was inter-schools racing, and swimming clubs would be on the lookout for new talent. If you were

spotted the club representative would approach your family with an invitation for you to join their club.

At 13 years I started at Kewdale High which was huge, a two storey building with an outdoor swimming pool of 25 metres, a gym, tennis court, and an 'Oval' – a sportsfield on which all field games were played, such as cricket, football, and Aussie rules soccer.

I was reasonably successful in my chosen sport of swimming and eventually held some state records for the butterfly and backstroke but I gave it up because I wanted more of a social life.

Deborah Simpson (née Style)

FOOTBALL AND CRICKET

Joint Effort.

There was a senior girls school at Tindal Street but the senior boys joined us at Clifton Road in about 1930–31. Tindal Street boys thought they were superior to us because they came from Moseley rather than Balsall Heath. One good thing that came of Tindal amalgamating with us was that we had a better football team

Boys' Football Team. 1913–1914.

42

with the better players from both schools. We didn't win any medals but we did quite well. I won a medal for the high jump at the school sports day the year before I left in 1932.
Jack Billington

A National Sport.
St. Kitts, West Indies.
Cricket was part of the culture; every part of the island had a cricket team. We were never short of a game to watch – free of charge. You simply sat down and watched. We kids were free to roam the island, we could go any place we wanted and were always considered to be safe. I was a bowler then as I am now, playing games with the kids around here (Balsall Heath 2008) teaching them the techniques of cricket and football. I think that Sandy Point's uniform, brown shorts, blue and white striped top, identified not only the school but also the area of the island to which we belonged.
Errol Thomas

The Undulating Pitch.
Meadows Primary School.
We made the short trip from Northfield to Shenley Park Fields for football and cricket. To this day, people don't believe my description of the football pitches at Shenley Park. They were marked out on and over undulating ground, in fact over mounds. If you were on the wing with the ball and wanted to cross it into the centre you might not have been able to kick the ball because it ran away from you so fast downhill. Taking a penalty was tricky, as the spot seemed to be level with the cross-bar!
Chris Sutton

A Smashing Time.
My dad had got me some glasses which I wore for about two minutes. I was playing football and this kid hit the ball and smashed them. I got laughed at but I was scared of telling my dad as he had only just got them.
Sohail Yousef

Natural Selection.
When it came to being selected for team sports, it was a case that if you were good at football, you were considered to be good at everything else. Don't know how it worked, but Perry Beeches Secondary School Cricket team was full of footballers! Because I was good at swimming, I was an automatic choice for canoeing. I reckon

my selection was based on the principle that if I turned the canoe over, I could swim for my life.
Peter Cole

Talking To Pictures.
Clifton Road Infants and Dennis Road Secondary Modern 1950's and 60's.
I was a bit sporty as a lad, there was cricket and football and I did some running. I picked up medals for these on annual sports days, and also took part, as a supporter, in local inter-school competition swimming. I remember the crowd sitting in the balcony seats at Moseley Road swimming baths cheering their favourites on.

In recent times while doing some voluntary work I had to go and see the headmaster at Anderton Park School – the former Dennis Road. Adorning a flight of stairs leading to his office was a host of old school photographs, and among them pictures of school cricket and football teams of the past. I was delighted to find one in which I featured. Anyone nearby would have been amused as I talked to myself and the photographs as I discovered and named old school friends.

In 1958 my sporting interests led to my being picked with others to represent the school at a memorial service to those who died in the Munich air disaster. It took place at St John's Church, Sparkhill; the congregation included a number of well-known footballers of the time.
John William Brown.

All Work.
Ghana, Africa, 1970's and 80's.
The compound housed a large football pitch, but I was not very interested in sport. I remember trying football and not being very successful at it. I was, I consider, rather a weakling. On Saturday mornings I'd get up very early and go to the library to study, and by the time I had finished studying around noon the game period was over.
Peter Owusu

Sporty Or Cool.
Nairobi, Kenya, 1980's and 90's.
I don't remember participating much in sport until high school. We played football for 55 minutes of our hour lunch-break, going back into school for afternoon classes, all dirty and sweaty. Later we gave that up as we didn't want to be dirty and messy any more. We wanted instead to be thought of as "cool".

One year, I didn't participate in events on sports day, but felt I had to go to support my fellow house members. I soon regretted being there, being baked by the scorching Kenya sun, no water, and no shade, nothing. I simply dropped off, and missed most of it.

Rizwan Janmohamed

Sport And Harsh Winters.
Wyoming Country Schooling.

What Thermopolis and most High-Schools in America were into in a big way was sport. Thermopolis had a 1st and 2nd team in both Basketball and American Football, Baseball was not prominent at all. The harsh winter dictated when each sport was played. American football was played from term opening in September through to December and Basketball from December to March.

Ron Vannelli

HOCKEY

Girls' Hockey Team in the 1930's.

Water lilies.

From Camp Hill we used to go to play sports at Vicarage Road. If you were like me and didn't like hockey, you stood at the back so you didn't get picked to play. Then you could wander round the gardens instead. There was a big pond in front of the Cartland's house and I remember picking some water lilies and taking them home with me.

Betty Thornicroft

Lost Teeth, Kept Friend.
Leigh, Lancashire, late 40's, early 50's.

I remember playing hockey at school and we were told not to raise the sticks too high – that is not to raise them above the shoulder. I got too excited and knocked out the two front teeth of my best friend Brenda Rigby. We spent the rest of the afternoon searching the grass for her teeth which she carried home crying! We stayed good friends though.

Marian Dimulias (née Brown)

The Netball Team from Heath Mount School, Balsall Heath, rejoicing on winning the South Birmingham Schools' District Cup in the 1980's.

Sport for the Posh.

Wakefield High didn't play Netball, that was a 'working class' game. My mother told me of a French game she had played while at the school. It was called Lacrosse, involving a court with a net, a ball and a hand carried net, fishing-like. This had disappeared from the curriculum by the time I was a pupil, the main team game being Hockey. Being the complete swot I played only when forced. One time I thought that the long jump might be a sports activity that would suit me. It didn't look too difficult so I gave it a try, and wrecked my knee.

Joyce Ashworth

ATHLETICS

Short cut.

I certainly didn't take to athletics and the annual cross-country race held in January was to be avoided at all costs. It was almost mandatory to take part. I took to hiding myself in the school buildings for much of the race, joining in with the main pack of runners for the last lap.

Selina Brown

TEACHERS

The Battle Axe.
Clifton Road, 1930's.

Miss Anderton was a character. She wore a skirt down to the ground and regularly hitched it up to retrieve her purse from a pocket in her petticoat. Miss Newey took the top class and was, I believe, the Deputy Head or Chief Assistant as they were known at that time. Miss Cooper was something of a battle-axe; an extremely formidable person indeed and a stickler for discipline. She was one of the old uncertificated teachers of whom a few remained in Birmingham. I remember that we feared Miss Cooper and I was greatly relieved when for some reason or other I by-passed her class.

Jack Harris

Headphones Under The Hair.
St Alban's School, 1920's.

My only memory of a teacher in the infants was a Miss Macevern who taught us when we were in the last class there. I probably remember her because of her hairstyle of two lengths of plaited hair taken over and down each side of her head and wound in two circles which covered her ears. I think it was known as the earphone style. Miss Macevern kept in touch with some of us long after we had left her class, inviting us once to her rooms which she occupied in a house on Moseley Road near Highgate Place. She had been to Italy for a holiday and she wanted to show us photographs that she had taken of the towns and countryside.

Len Baron

TEACHER: "NOW IF WE TAKE AWAY THE FIRST THREE, WHAT HAVE WE LEFT?"
FATHER'S BOY: "ALSO RANS, TEACHER!"

A Maths lesson. 1927.

Fair Teacher.

Upper Highgate St School, 1900's.

When I was six years old I was in Miss Bowman's class. She was very slight and always seemed very busy. Her dress was always immaculate. She usually wore a black skirt and white blouse with a bow tied at the neck. She was rather strict but I liked her because she was fair and had no favourites.

Nell Wilkins

Keep Your Hair On.

For the first three years I was taught by Miss Rowe, who was quite small. I remember one day in the playground, Commonwealth Day, when we had to salute the flag; it was windy and her wig blew off. I had to catch it for her. She was most embarrassed and glad to have it back.

Winifred Berkeley

Honk! Honk!

Mr Heskey, general and boys PE, drove a Morris plywood bodied three wheeler car with one wheel at the rear. We boys loved to wait for him to drive into school in the morning, and shout after him – "Honk! Honk!"

Ron & Gladys Ford (née Woolley)

Women Worse Than Men.

Steward Street School.

All the male teachers were called up at the start of the war. So we had women teachers and I found they could be crueller than the men.

Ron Hubbell

From Father To Son.
Dennis Road, 1930's.

A Brushwork class at Dennis Rd School, Balsall Heath. Birmingham. 1891.

Before me, my father went to Dennis Road School soon after it opened, and I had one teacher, Mr Stone, who had also taught my father. He was quite old and grey by then and quite savage. We were all frightened of him.

One day in his class we were doing drawing and he came over to me. I really thought he was going to hit me but instead he reached out and touched my cheek saying, "That's very good." I thought, "Blimey!"
Maurice Cleaver

Not A Man's Job.
In those days it was a case that infant schools had all female teachers. The employment of male teachers in reception classes may have been something that

was frowned on; it may have been a hang-over from the war, or simply because of the age of the children – not a man's job. Whatever the case, it wasn't until junior school that I became aware of male teachers.

Joyce Ashworth

Wait For It, Wait For It!
St. Thomas C. of E.

In the senior school the headmaster had been a Sergeant-Major in the army. A little man, he always wore leather gloves and carried a small stick or baton under his arm. If he came upon you doing something he didn't like, such as mucking about, he would tap you with his baton while making his point about your behaviour. In retrospect it doesn't take much imagination to realise that women had been doing the majority of teaching while the war was in progress and that as the years went by more and more men would come available to the education system.

Pat Johnson (née Shine)

Blamed For Breaking.
Kingston, Jamaica.

None of the teachers at this school inspired me, and one of them I learned to hate. It was the headmaster. He gave me and the other black girl a science project to do. We had to measure rainfall and set up an instrument outside in the open to do this. It transpired that the instrument got broken, don't know how it broke, but it was not down to us. However when Mr Gooch found out, at assembly with the whole school present, he called out our names for us to stand up. He proceeded to give us the most awful dressing down in front of everybody. I think that was one of the worst times of my life. I hated him from that moment and still wonder how he could have done that to a child.

Marcia Vizor

The Uncommon Male Teacher Inspires.
Lucerne, Wyoming.

In Wyoming, during the early school years of lower level education, to have a male teacher was a rarity. It fact it may have been thought unethical to have them in pre-high school establishments. So when a male teacher came to Lucerne it was both a surprise and delight, and for us, good. He coached us in Basketball teaching us the fundamentals and the details. He set up a team and entered us in the local school league. Together with parents he organised transport to the venues. All round we were a great team. For a school at our level it would have been unusual to have a

Basketball team. He was in my estimation brilliant, and the influence to become a teacher myself.

Ron Vannelli

Cartoonist.

Moseley Road Art School.

The teachers wore black gowns but only for the academic subjects. They had mortar boards too but I don't remember them wearing them.

One of the staff was Norman Pett who was famous because he did the comic strip in the Daily Mirror under the name of "Jane". Actually it was really rather racy stuff. He used to sit at his desk in classes working away and we always thought he was doing his cartoons.

Maurice Cleaver.

A Picture Study class at St. Anne's School Chelmsford, Essex.

On The Edge.

At age eleven we arrived at Bishop Challoner RC. The face that was to become most familiar was that of the headmaster 'Wally' Welford. He was always immaculately dressed in his suit, stood very upright, and wore a moustache. He was very stern looking, and maintained a strict discipline. In assembly, he would stand on the stage with his toes hanging over the edge; we kids always thought that if he came any nearer the edge he would fall off.

In comparison, completely opposite to Mr Welford was our term class teacher Miss Mortimer. She was a young thing and we pre-adolescent boys thought she was very 'tasty'. She often dressed in a rolled necked sweater and wore a wide belt around her waist. We just couldn't take our eyes off her figure. I think most of the boys in the class had a crush on her and were jealous when we found out she was going out with one of the other teachers, Mr Cassidy, whom she eventually married.

Michael Henry Fitzpatrick

Lessons For Life.

Bishop Challoner, Kings Heath, 1940's and 50's.

Among these ex-army type teachers was a Mr Carr, about whom we kids got the idea that he was ex-commando. He was small in stature but big on discipline. One of the first things he said to us was, "You play ball with me and I'll play ball with you". This was his way of warning us about our behaviour in his class. Mr Clarke, the science teacher, taught us something about the world economy when he instilled the idea "Export or Die". The deputy-head, Miss Kelly who took the top class, gave us "Towels are for drying, not cleaning" in response to the state of the towels when us hoards were finished with them. The head himself, Mr Welford who always took the weekly assembly and taught us the song "Jerusalem", made us learn parrot-fashion the sentence, "Leave other people, and other people's property alone". This idea has always remained with me ever since those days in the mid fifties. It wouldn't be a bad motto for today's schools.

Reginald Arthur Brown

Startled Punk.

One teacher I remember because of her looks. She was to me a visual sensation with really bushy and frizzy hair like a startled punk.

Anjum Gul

Are You Listening?

The geography teacher could be cruel if he wanted to be. Not paying due attention could bring a piece of chalk flying through the air, hitting a pupil with the accuracy intended – on the ear. He would bellow after the throw; "Are you listening laddie?" At the same time he could be one of the boys, like the time he joined his pupils listening to a Test-Match commentary in class – I remember Ian Chappell and Greg Chappell were playing for Australia against England – on one of the boys' tranny (portable radio). This kind of "We're all boys together" attitude was highlighted by the example set by Mr Chapman, Maths, when he accepted his pupils challenge to "Stand on the bowling ball, sir" – he fell off, breaking his ankle.

One of the teachers was Mr Lea. Referring to the subject of being a pupil at the school, he told us that he felt sorry for us. Pressed to explain, he said; "At such a vital time in your life, to be stuck here in this environment – all male, macho – with its bullying overtones and no girls is not good". The school did begin to employ female teachers while I was still a pupil. A number of us found that we had more empathy with a female tutor and made more progress in a subject. The very first woman to teach at Kings Norton Grammar School was a Miss Ferraro, an English teacher. We boys with our overstimulated imagination, enthused about her, comparing her to 1970's sirens such as Racquel Welsh and TV's Charlie's Angels.

Chris Sutton

Studying Local History at Woodview School, Edgbaston, Birmingham. 2005.

Chapter 3

Trouble

Getting into trouble at school prompted many of the most strongly felt memories. The misdemeanours described don't really sound too dreadful though obviously ink was the bane of teachers' lives at one time. Parents, especially mums, seemed to have been active, though not always in support of their offspring.

Bullying was remembered by some as a major worry. A tide of resentment flows through these memories, that the teachers knew about it but either ignored or supported it.

However, such troubles pale into insignificance beside the chilling record of corporal punishment in "Six of the Best". It's also interesting to see that such memories come from many parts of the world. Such punishment did not become illegal in Britain until 1986 in state schools but was banned in America very much earlier.

It should come as a relief, then, to read memories of schools taking active steps to ensure the health of their pupils but here, as well, people remember not so much benevolence and goodwill as pain, fear and misery!

PLAYING UP

Playing Truant.
Sometimes in the last year, we would wag some sessions and go to my friend's house to watch music videos, but that wasn't often. Some pupils would drink alcohol or take drugs at school. It became the norm. Some girls I knew got pregnant towards the end of school and had to leave.
Ally Sultana

Don't Sit At The Back.
Rushcliffe, Nottingham, 1990's.
The worst thing I did was to bunk-off lessons, some classes were simply boring, or far too long in terms of time. If my friends and I didn't want to attend, we would bunk-off while still at school. We would hide in the toilets and have a smoke. We were not too experienced smokers and we were always telling each other to "Suck it! Suck it!"

I do remember one serious episode of indiscipline leading to the school bus, which was hired, being taken out of service permanently because of pupils' unruly behaviour. They lifted the seating from the back of the vehicle and threw it out via the emergency exit.

Selina Brown

Inky Tricks.
Cheshire 1920's.
We used to have pens with nibs. I was caught playing darts on the blackboard with the pens.

Gwen White

In Trouble.
Our desks all had inkwells of course and I remember soaking up the blotting paper and flicking it across the room.

I also got into trouble for hitting other children and was disapproved of for being a tomboy. On one occasion in particular I remember feeling very upset as my grandmother had died and I was feeling angry. I hit a boy and got into trouble. No one asked why.

Anita Halliday

Ink Maid.
Clifton Road.
I had the job of filling the ink wells. One day I dropped a big bottle of ink all over the sink. Luckily there was not much in it at the time and I was able to clean the sink with lots of water. I was dripping wet when I had finished and the teacher gave me a ticking off for being so clumsy.
Sheila Reynolds (née Moore)

Straw Darts.
Glebe Farm Park, Stechford.
We boys made papier mache projectiles which were flicked from the end of a ruler. Pen nibs were broken in two so that we were left with two separate little points. Then, when we had first break in the morning, we took the straws which were intended for drinking from our free bottles of milk and attached our points and used them as darts.

On two consecutive Wednesday afternoons I played truant, sneaking off behind the shops to drag on a fag. Then on one of the following Mondays I came home from school and wondered where my mother was as she would normally be in the yard doing the washing on that day of the week. As I walked into the house I was met with a big leather belt from behind the door. "What have you been doing playing the wag?" she demanded. The school-board man had been to the house.
Ron Ford

They Shall Not Meet.
The boys were in a separate part of the school from the girls and the playground had a dividing wall. Communication was forbidden, but very often the boys climbed on top of the wall and shouted at us girls – disgusting behaviour! As I had three brothers with friends, I was often told off for being too friendly with the boys.
Emily Jones (née Belcher)

The American Way.
Bronx, New York, 1980's.
Halloween celebrations are a big tradition out there, with people dressing-up as ghouls and the like, trick and treating at people's homes and other public places. The dark side to this could be witnessed when students had things such as eggs and flour thrown at them at the exit from school. Sinisterly sometimes hair remover would be included in the missiles. The girls in particular were mostly ready for this by wearing hoods and carrying umbrellas. These instances have in the past, escalated out of hand and led to more than one death over the years.
Samantha Hines

Paper The Ceiling.
Loxton Street Juniors, Nechells, 1940's.
Some of us kids used to collect fag (cigarette) packets; not unusual for the time of course as the cigarette companies produced picture cards to be collected. We also stripped the light tissue paper from the foil found in the packs, twisting it on our fingers to form cups. We then wetted and threw them up at the classroom ceiling where they stuck and stayed for a long time.
Dennis Hammond

Playground Trouble.
One friend whose name I do remember, Robert Brown, was the proverbial blonde haired, blue eyed lad – there always seemed to be one around – whom teachers seem to take to. We fell out one day and started fighting in the playground. Somehow he emerged from the episode as the good guy and was rewarded by the headmistress with a model or mock-up of a Red Indian canoe. "See" he said later "it was your fault." I was the bad boy again. Another friend that I had a playground rumble with was a Shea Bartley. He gave me a smack in the jaw and knocked several of my bottom teeth out. I think they must have been ready to come out as they did come out so readily.
Michael Henry Fitzpatrick

Raining Bits and Pieces.
Ysgol Y Gadr, Wales.
I used to be involved in a lot of pranks such as making little flying objects that you used to be able to stick to the ceiling of the Assembly Hall. Every so often they would fall down and drop on people.
Stephen Gwynne

Boat Builder.
Bristol 1960's.
As boy and girl twins we must have been a handful for teachers to deal with. I remember that when he was naughty and got into trouble, I would start crying and get him off. But it wasn't always him being naughty, I could do just as well. One misdemeanour of mine led to me having to stand motionless facing the perimeter wall in the playground with my friends playing games around me. I had been in the toilet block making paper boats from the toilet tissue and sailing them in the hand basin.
Marion Ridsdill

No dancing on these desks.

Dancing On The Desks.
Glebe Farm Park, Stechford.
I remember the school desks were made in pairs, doubled up, so two pupils sat together in one unit. When the teacher was absent for a moment, we would climb up on them and walk across them skipping from one desk to another, or we might try to jump over them. One day I fell and crashed face first into one of the desks, cutting an eyebrow. I thought the teacher, Mr Smith, might cut the other one for me, but no, he was kind and took me to the headmaster to get me fixed up. Mr Bradbury said they had better let my parents know about my accident but fearing the worse from them, I said "Do you have to?"
Gladys Ford (née Woolley)

BULLYING

The Biggest Bully.
Woodfall School, Cheshire.
I remember the headmaster, Dicky Duncer, standing up and saying, "There's only one bully in this school.... me".
Bob Greenway

Country Bumpkin.
I won a scholarship to Camp Hill School but it was very hard starting there. Most of my primary schooldays had been spent at the village school in Wythall and the

other girls at Camp Hill called me a country bumpkin. Most of them were from posh families who were paying fees so I was looked down on as a scholarship girl. On one occasion we had been dissecting worms in our Biology class and I found I had got one of them in my lunch time sandwiches.
Betty Thornicroft

Grading for Bullies.
Kings Norton Grammar School. 1970's.
Bullying was commonplace within the class, not necessarily across classes unless it was older boys taking advantage of the younger ones. Grading of pupils was done via the 11+ results and a set of tests we took on arrival. These tests were not difficult, it would have been hard to fail them. We were graded A, B, or C. Puzzlingly C was top grade. If you were in the top grade, or bottom grade, you could be the target of bullies. Teachers at the school were, in my view, always aware of the bullying but turned a blind eye.
Chris Sutton

Don't Pick On Me!
What I did find interesting was the ethos of the school. When you first started you were called a fag; in the first year of the school you were a servant for the older kids.
    They picked on the wrong person. I wasn't going to do that and not use anyone else either, and after that they didn't. They were quite horrible. They used to put their heads down the toilets and flush them, which was cruel. I didn't like the idea of anyone being taken advantage of. But we didn't do it and nobody else did it when they got older, so that tradition fizzled out.
Pam Mullin

Seriously Useful.
Because I was a very serious person as a child I used to get bullied quite a lot. But it was nice when all the rest of the kids used to come up and ask me for help with their homework.
Sukaina Khimji

Loved for My Brother.
I just missed out on going to Bournville Grammar School, failing the 11+ exam, but I did make the top class of Turves Green Girls Comprehensive School. I found the all girl school seemed to foster bitchiness among the pupils. There was underlying social segregation into groups. On one side the studious ones which today we would call Geeks. On the other, the 'Wild-Bunch', who pretty much

pleased themselves. I was one of those in limbo between the two groups, except that a lot of the girls were interested in me because I was the sister of Robin Hall. My brother was four years older than me and a pupil at Turves Green Boys just up the road from our school. The girls said that he was the best thing they had ever seen.

Sally Williams (née Hall)

PARENTS

Mum Didn't Help.
Clifton Road.
I remember one day Mr H. threw a board rubber at someone but it missed and hit me in the face so I went home with a black eye. My mum came storming up to the school and had a go at the teacher. You didn't cross my mum. But from that day my time in his class was a misery.

Anne Hill (née Graham)

Mum Did Help.
Clifton Road.
I was caught by a Miss Wallace playing ball in the classroom and had the ball confiscated. When my mother, who was barely five feet, heard this she marched to the Headmistress and demanded its return – it had cost one penny! She came away triumphant.

Emily Jones (née Belcher)

Don't Mess With My Mum.
In primary school, the main thing that sticks out is my mother. One time the teacher gave me bruises and my mother went over to the school and gave him a good leathering. He didn't bother me after that.

Jim Atkinson

Homework!
At one point the headmistress decided we would have homework. Now besides working as a slaughter-man in Newbury and running the local public house, my father had a smallholding with a number of animals. When he saw what homework I had to do, he went to the school and told them I was much too busy to do homework. So that was the end of that!

Peter Davis

Mum To The Rescue.

I had wanted to learn to play the recorder and had borrowed one owned by the school. The teacher wanted me to give it back and so much did she insist that I gave it up. My mother went to see her. Their talk ended with my mother throwing the recorder at the teacher. I was not flavour of the month after that and always last to be given attention in her class.

Peter Cole

Listen up!

This particular teacher threatened us while holding up a pair of scissors, "I'll cut your ears off, if you don't behave." My mom came to the school to talk to her about the threat and she told my mom that the threat was only towards bad children and that I was not one of those. I was OK about her after that.

Samantha Hines

A mother's visit to school. 1909.

SIX OF THE BEST

Harsh Discipline.
1900's.

The teaching staff at the School for the Blind were very strict. I remember when I was about six or seven years of age that a teacher named Mrs Morley became very angry with me when I made some bad mistakes due to lack of concentration. She caught hold of my collar and paraded me around the playground while walloping me on my backside. I shall never forget it.

Albert Eaton

Dunce.
Conway School.

I remember I had to stand outside in the corridor facing the wall with a Dunce's cap on at Conway. I also had the cane, but I can't remember why I was being punished.

Yvonne Rollins (née Stead)

Bruised.
Clifton Road.
I was slapped on the back of the thighs by a teacher who was an ex-WAAF and she left lots of bruises and finger marks and made me stand in the corner. It was because none of us were in our seats. We all ran the wrong way and I ended up in the wrong place and got slapped. My mum came to school and complained. I went in to see the headmistress with her but I don't remember an apology.
Victoria Jeffs

Missiles.
The blackboard arrangements brought the blackboard ruler, a ready weapon for chastising the unruly, and if you were out of reach of the ruler there was always the missile of chalk to wake you up or cut your chatter.
Reginald Arthur Brown

Getting Caned.
1930's.
The cane was the most common form of discipline at school. It wasn't unusual for a boy to get four strokes on each hand which was very painful. A twelve inch ruler wasn't nearly as painful as a two foot cane. Charlie Cook, who lived in the same

Caning.

yard as me, was waiting in the school corridor to be caned for some misdeed or other. He moved the hands of the clock and put it forward so we left school a quarter of an hour early. He was caned for that too.

The teachers would also send letters home to your family for bad behaviour. In my case this would result in me getting a belting from my father or my mother would cane me herself with a cane she kept by the fireside for this purpose. When no-one was looking I used to 'smoke' the cane by burning it on the fire so it reduced inch by inch. When it was too small to use my mother sent me to Meacham's, the hardware store, to buy a new one for tuppence. She told me to get a good strong one.
Bernard Jackson

The Strap.
Scotland.
I got the strap in Scotland. It was on your hand and the strap was cut at the bottom. I got it for being five minutes late for school. I was about thirteen.
Dawn McGhie

Take A Message.
I remember one teacher at Dennis Road School who called me over one morning and asked me to go the shop during the lunch break on my way home. He wanted me to buy him a teacher's cane and gave me the money.

When I came back with it he said, "Hold out your hand". I did so and he whacked me with it hard. Then he said, "I expect you're wondering why I did that? Well, I found out that a friend of yours who's a real cause of trouble is joining this class so I want you to tell him that I've got this cane and that I'm prepared to use it!"
Maurice Cleaver

One Stroke Of The Cane.
When it came to discipline I think St Thomas's was much the same as any comparable school around. Caning was commonplace. I got the stick myself for talking in the line of children waiting to be called into our class. After being picked out for this misdemeanour, I had to stay at the front of the class so as to receive one stroke of the cane while everybody else sat at their desks.
Pat Johnson (née Shine)

Affronted Dignity.
One day my world fell apart, for though I could compose an essay with ease, I could not set it down neatly. After several mild scoldings for untidy work I was made to stand before the whole class and be publicly rebuked for not even trying to improve

it. I realise now that he tweaked one of my ringlets in playful though exasperated mood, but my dignity was further affronted by the laughter of the other children.
Valerie Harris (née Farrant)

The Sideburn Pull.
Dennis Road School, 1950's.

I recall one teacher in particular for his discipline methods. He would, as he walked around the class, come up behind us where we sat at our desk and take hold of our sideburns in his fingers, twisting and pulling upwards. We would naturally rise to ease the pain, and then with a grimace he commanded "Sit down, sit down" while we let out the exclamation "Ahhh – sir…"
Maurice Arthur Evans

Even Outside School You Could Get In Trouble…

One afternoon on our way home from school and playing football with a stone we accidentally hit a shop window, making a small hole. We quickly made ourselves scarce but the next morning the Headmaster summoned from the classroom all those who went that way home and paraded us in front of, to use his own words, "a man in blue". Perhaps because we owned-up and were truthful we escaped with a lecture, instructed to inform our parents and heard nothing more about the matter.
Alan Hemming

Frequent Use.

The worst memory I have is of the frequent use of the cane. It was not just used for disciplining pupils, but also if we made a mistake in our class or homework. We lived in constant dread of getting anything wrong. A boy in our class was told that if you laid a horse hair across your palm it would split the cane. One day he did this and we all watched hoping it would work, but of course it didn't.
Valerie Ganderton

"Give me a sentence with that word in it."
"The seat of my trousers is worn out but notwithstanding."

In trouble again. 1929.

Six Of The Very Best And A Good Report.

Robert Brown and I often cycled home together from Kings Heath to Balsall Heath. At one point in our journey, Park Hill School in Moseley, there was a manned school crossing. We often found ourselves racing down hill and reluctant to stop even when the lollipop man was stepping out on to the road. Our behaviour was noted and we were eventually caught and found out, though we had given false names and addresses.

Hauled before the headmaster at a full school assembly, he gave me six strokes of the cane. As he prepared to strike me each time, he asked a question "What is this for?" I answered "Disrespectful language." Then I held the other hand out, and he asked again "What is this for?" This time I answered "Giving a false identity"; and so it went on until my punishment was complete. He then told me to go and stand in the corner where I put my tingling hands on the cool wall. In the next moment I fainted and collapsed to the floor. I remember a voice shouting "Don't pick him up, don't pick him up" which I presume was the headmaster's. I was however picked up and taken out of the assembly hall.

I made no fuss about this of course, we didn't in those days, I certainly did not tell my mother, as that would likely lead to my getting another whack! It all blew over and some time later I received my school leaving report. I was amazed to read "Michael Fitzpatrick is an upstanding and reliable, intelligent person." I couldn't believe it, and thought they must have mixed me up with someone else.
Michael Henry Fitzpatrick

Discipline by Community Consent.
Wyoming Country Schooling.
There was no hard discipline at the school; corporal punishment was, even then, late 1940's, illegal. A teacher, as far as I was aware, never laid a hand on a kid. In the small community neither was it necessary. Parents were totally behind teachers, if you told your parents you had been in trouble at school, you would likely get it in the neck from them.
Ron Vannelli

Frightened.
In Maths class I was sat at the front and often as I stared out of the window day dreaming, a piece of chalk would hit me at the side of my head, or the blackboard rubber would zoom past close to me. On one occasion at least the teacher sneaked up quietly and slammed the board rule so hard on the desk that I was frightened out of my wits.
Marcia Vizor

Struck Down By Religion.
On one occasion as the class was making its way down to the church for a service, I was playing up. The teacher came behind me and smacked me over the head

with a big book. I don't think it was a Bible. However I collapsed on the spot. I may have fainted for a moment or two, but picked myself up. The incident caused quite a commotion and the teacher involved must have been worried as he offered me his cup of tea at break-time.

Michael Henry Fitzpatrick

No Regrets for Punishment.
Sandy Point Primary, St. Kitts, West Indies, 1960's.

I remember the strictness of this school and I think that it reflected the social discipline of the whole of St Kitts Island. For instance there was punishment for being late for school. This could take the form of a chore, such as sweeping the playground, or you could be beaten with the Tamarind Whip, made from a thin branch of the Tamarind tree. The police used a similar method of punishment; it was possible to be whipped as an alternative to prison. I find that I am happy that I grew up under such a regime of strictness. A good education was made more likely by it, but also I believe it helped me later in life to survive, to respect and get on with other people.

Errol Thomas

Choice.

I remember one of my teachers who had a slipper called Percy which he kept in a glass case at the front of the class. On one occasion the whole class were to be punished so he offered us a choice...... Percy or 100 lines in detention? We all made our choices. Then he said, "Right. All those who chose detention line up now for Percy and all those who chose Percy will do detention."

Russ Spring

"HARD LINES!" 18/2

Hard Lines.

Who Burnt the Smokers' Home?
Kings Norton Grammar School.

Discipline was something simply expected and part of the environment of the school; canings if necessary were the responsibility of the two deputy heads. Mostly though, punishments consisted of detention. A great example of this was after the Cricket Pavilion

was burnt down by a stray firework, a rocket. A number of pupils were kept back every school night for three weeks in an attempt to get the culprit.
Chris Sutton

Language Of Punishment.
Church School, Madhya Pradesh, Northern India.
About twenty years ago I went to a British Catholic school in Madhya Pradesh where discipline was very harsh and corporal punishment was considered normal. The Principal was a French nun. She used to hit the boys with her belt when they were rude and a typical punishment for forgetting homework was getting the stick on the front of the hand. It was important to always speak English in class and when the Principal caught anyone talking in Hindi or another language, she made them eat two or three spoonfuls of Neem chutney, which is very bitter and made the eyes and nose run. Neem chutney is used in Ayurverdic medicine for skin complaints. It is taken orally but only in very small doses.
Nisha Sharma

Good Or Bad.
Budapest, 1980's.
Discipline was maintained by psychological rather than physical abuse. The head would storm into a class shouting and banging doors. Children would be sent to detention for not dressing correctly, having untidy hair, or being a few minutes late for school. There was a big red – Soviet influence red – board in the corridor where photographs of pupils that had received awards for their work were pinned up as an example to the rest of the school. Children who were sent to detention for some misdemeanour would be made to stand in the corridor next to the red board. I once found myself in detention standing next to this board with a photo of myself having received an academic award. Seems I was both good and bad at the same time.
Laura Szendy

Cane Or Pump?
Kings Heath Technical School, 1980's.
When I moved up to Kings Heath Technical School for Boys I found the discipline regime was of the strictest order. We would be physically punished for not paying attention in class. It wasn't simply a question of getting the cane; some teachers used footwear in the form of a pump whacking us with it on the backside. In carrying out the punishment a teacher would take a running jump, bringing the pump crashing down on our backside in order to slap us as hard as possible.
John Bealt

Lying down for Punishment.
Ghana, 1970's and 80's.
We were caned for being late for the start of the school day. At assembly teachers would stand by the doors and note the names of late comers. One teacher, Mr Asiedu, when he went out of the classroom on some school business and found an unruly and noisy class on his return would stand by the door and announce "I will beat the whole class." We would then all have to lie down on the tables and he would beat our backsides.
Peter Owusu

Getting The Stick.
Nairobi, Kenya, 1980's and 90's.
Our primary school in Nairobi was, in reflection, rather secular. We were frightened to get on the wrong side of the African teachers in particular as they generally were the first to use the stick for almost any misdemeanour. We were struck on the palm of the hand like most others, but sometimes we were forced to have a pencil 'weaved' through our fingers so that some of our fingers were raised to intensify the pain as the stick rained down on hands. I can still remember having a swollen thumb after such treatment.
Rizwan Janmohamed

IN SICKNESS AND IN HEALTH

Checking The Spots.
Clifton Road School.
My daughter had measles and the School Board man came round to check that she had spots.
Rose Pearson

The Board Man.
Cheshire, 1920's.
We were off school sick with chicken pox, me and my brother, and the School Board man came round to check up. We all hid under the table.
Gwen White

Cod Liver Oil.
Open Air School, Birmingham.
I used to dread the morning. We had cod liver oil.
Olive Dowdeswell (née Rose)

Too Ill To Be Ill.

Things were not good from the start at Albert Bradbeer Primary. The Headmistress was always on to me about something; mainly I think it was about my missing school so much. I was a sickly child and often off school with a sore throat or other complaint. I was thin with it, which brought on name calling from the other children, such as skinny and twiggy. I was also teased about my Yorkshire accent. My friend's brother would repeat every word I said. When I did get back to school after a bout of illness, teachers made sarcastic comments about lost time – surely I couldn't be that ill etc. It got to the point where I was physically sick at the very thought of going back to school after having lost time again.

Sally Williams (née Hall)

The Infamous Nurse.
St. Thomas C of E.

We had regular health inspections, the famous nit nurse, the dentist and eye tests. I was never given a card to inform my mother that I had nits thankfully, but I did have an eye problem, an astigmatism which ran in the family.

Pat Johnson (née Shine)

The Paraffin Rinse.
Early 20th Century.

We had a medical inspection when first starting school. Eyes, ears and teeth were examined and any problems were dealt with at the school clinic. Then, every morning, we had a hygiene inspection for hands and finger nails. Also shoes were inspected. If you didn't pass you were rapped on the knuckles with a ruler. The nit nurse came to Clifton school regularly. Most of the children had 'dirty heads' and were sent home to have their hair soaked in paraffin. If we had long hair it was plaited.

Mrs Osborne

The "Nit Nurse" at Heath Mount School, Balsall Heath, Birmingham. 1980's.

Mobile Showers At Mary Street.

At some time in the early 1940's I can remember mobile shower trailers coming to Mary Street School and being positioned on the far side of the playground. Whatever the reason was for the showers, it was certainly a novelty for the majority of us who came from homes without bathrooms. We had medical inspections at various times and I recall with horror having teeth extracted at the school clinic at Sherbourne Road School. There was also a school clinic in Severn Street, which I attended for foot exercises.

Alan Hemming

Down In The Mouth.

We had regular visits from the school dentist. If you were found to need treatment you were given an appointment to go to Sherbourne Road clinic – a place which struck dread into the heart of every school child in the area. We also had regular visits from the nit nurse.

Anne Hemming (née Davis)

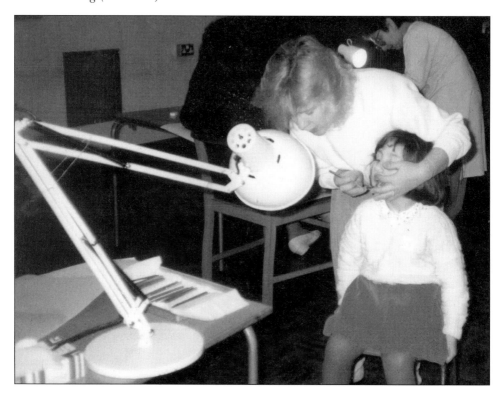

Dental Inspection in the classroom at Heath Mount School, Balsall Heath. 1980's.

Rubber Masks And Blood.

The Sherbourne Road Dental Clinic was a vile place with rows of chairs ready for those to be treated. I remember having a rubber gas mask over my face when I had a tooth out. When you came round you were given a tin mug of salt water and you had to spit it out into one of a long row of sinks, so you not only saw the blood you were spitting out, but everyone else's as well. There was even blood on the wall. It put me off going to the dentist for life.

Diane Stead

TB Vaccination.

I was vaccinated at school including the BCG vaccination for Tuberculosis. Unfortunately all ours went wrong and we all had badly infected arms which took a long time to heal.

Bron Salway (née Jones)

TB.

Friars School, Bangor.

I was vaccinated at school. We all lined up to have it done, but it didn't stop me getting Tuberculosis later in life.

Pete Salway

Polio.

The big scare when I was at primary school was Polio. We had one girl who caught it and she eventually came to school with a paralysed arm which filled me with terror. Anyway, at last, polio vaccination was arranged but there was something wrong with it. Another girl and I had paralysed legs for a week afterwards. They told us they had sent the batch back for checking but we didn't ever hear the outcome.

Val Hart

Break Time.

My best friend broke her arm on the trampoline but the teacher wouldn't believe her and made her keep going. She was just standing on the trampoline and crying. She eventually went to hospital and they found she had indeed broken her arm.

Helen Donaghy

Chapter 4

Happy Days

Tests and exams were obviously a well remembered challenge. From the 1944 Education Act secondary provision was divided into Grammar, Secondary Modern and Technical Schools. Entry to Grammar School was achieved by passing the 11+ exam but passing this exam or, indeed, one at 13+ for entry to Technical School, did not mean that places were taken up. Family circumstances sometimes intervened.

The rest of this section is a lot happier. Rewards and prizes were valued and appreciated as well as the opportunities to take part in special events, school plays and trips. These must be some of the happiest memories in the book and a pride in achievement shines out from the pages. Playground games were good, too. They present a picture of co-operation and friendship, vividly recalled.

School meals, however, get a very mixed bag of memories. Someone going to school from the age of five to sixteen would have eaten about 2000 school dinners. Small wonder, then, that they evoke such strong memories both for good and bad. "Chocolate concrete" was tops but down the bottom of the ratings was the dreaded "frog spawn" and lumpy mashed potato. However, it's also interesting to see that some children from different cultural backgrounds really enjoyed the English food because it was different.

WINNERS AND LOSERS

Testing Times.
Brainy, Medium Or Stupid.
Loxton Street Juniors.
Pupils were graded by academic ability. It was possible to be promoted or relegated from stream to stream, 'A, B or C'. We kids had different terminology for this grading; 'brainy', 'medium', and 'stupid'. Mind you, you had to be pretty smart to escape to grammar school. We were plebs (from the lower class) and were therefore given a basic education. That was the way it was; the same for all of us except, that is, for the talented few.
Dennis Hammond

Intelligence Tests.

Un-trendy is not a word to use for the times, 1940's and 50's, but it would have described Lawfield's philosophy on education. In this inner city roughish school, there were no frills. The aim was to get those who were capable, a scholarship (a forerunner of the 11+) in the three R's. The top classes were trained for exams, taking mock papers on a weekly basis. Entry to the top echelons for pupils was by way of an intelligence test, a method considered to filter-out the brighter boy or girl. Head teachers were competitive as the schools built their reputation on the results.

Don't let the Standards slip.

Joyce Ashworth

Pass Or Stay.
Ghana, Africa, 1970's and 80's.

In the primary school we progressed from class one to class six by the passing of exams. If you didn't pass the end of term exam, you didn't pass to the next class. This happened to me in my first year as I had to miss some of my schooling due to an abscess I had in an un-mentionable place. But I did make up ground later. In one particular exam the English teacher gave us an essay to write and when he had marked our scripts and was handing them back to us, he said to me, "Your father has a son". This was his way of complimenting me on my work.

Peter Owusu

Making The Grade.
New York.

To progress through grades you had to earn credits, most of these came from taking S.A.T.S (Aptitude Tests) in all subjects, that is everything from the academic, through sports, and up to, and including folk dancing. I failed a gym class but picked up credits for being early in the morning at school to study. If you didn't get enough credits, you simply did not move up. I had often wondered at the fact there were boys/men bigger than my big brother in my class. I came to realise that they had not moved up as they should have, and it was inevitable that they would drop-out as others had before them.

Samantha Hines

AWARDS AND PRIZES

Attendance Medal awarded to Annie Pitt. 1906.

Never a Day Missed.

I spent all of my schooldays at Clifton Road School. I have my bronze and silver medals for never losing a day at school except for the one allowed for the Sunday School outing.

Jack Billington

Lost Opportunity.

When I returned to Birmingham after the war I went back to my old school, Christchurch C.E, for the last year. Mr Bayliss, the headmaster, asked if my friend and I would like to sit the Grammar School exam and we both passed. At home we were not very well off at all and it was decided that we could not afford for me to take my place. Mr Bayliss came to our house and stressed that it was an opportunity not to be missed, but to no avail. He talked to me in his office and said how sorry he was. I left school at 14 with a great report of which I was very proud.

Patricia Green (née Rowbotham)

Escapism.
St. George's Primary School, Wallasey.

The days of the 11 plus arrived, or the Scholarship, as it was called. I remember a feeling of excitement at this different day or two: it was fun to sit in a different desk

and not have proper lessons, and I wrote a composition about "A day in the life of a budgie" when I escaped from my cage!
Wendy Beynon (née Forsyth)

Congratulations.
Every Friday we did a handwriting exercise and the best few went on the wall for a week. Once a year at exam time long tables were arranged in a rectangle round the hall and practical maths questions were placed on them, weighing, measuring etc., which we thought was quite a treat. The year I left Mary Street four of us passed for the Grammar School. One boy went to King Edward's Camp Hill. Another boy, myself and my friend Dorothy went to Waverley Grammar School in Small Heath. I still have the letter of congratulations which I received from the Head of Mary Street, Miss Bentley.
Anne Hemming (née Davis)

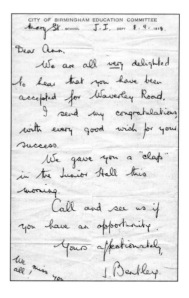

Congratulations! You've passed the 11+ exam. Letter to Anne Hemming. 1948.

No Choice.
I progressed OK in this atmosphere of learning and won prizes of books for reading. But, when it came to the 11+ St Thomas's staff advised my mother that I was not up to the standard required and shouldn't be entered for the exam. My brother on the other hand was considered (I agree) very, very clever and was put forward for the exam. My mother later said that at the time she wasn't given a choice about my educational options. She had, she said, often wished that she had ignored the school's advice.
Pat Johnson (née Shine)

Passed!
At about the age of thirteen I recall going to Golden Hillock Road School, Small Heath, to sit the Technical School Entrance Exam. I was the only one of my group to pass and was offered a place at Bordesley Green Technical School. However, due to family financial circumstances at that time, I was unable to take up the offer. My school friends thought I wasn't going because no one else had passed. I could not tell them the real reason.
Alan Hemming

Getting Into Art.
Moseley Road Art School.
One day at Dennis Road School a teacher said to me, "You really ought to sit the exam for the Art School, you know". This exam was like the one for grammar school and included writing a composition, for example, as well as a lot of art. I went along to the school itself to take the exam and managed to pass.
Maurice Cleaver

Parent :—(sternly) "Well, what do you think of this disgusting school report?" Tommy :—(indignantly) "I reckon it's a good case for libel !"

The Day of Reckoning. 1941.

Good Pupil And A Teacher.
Clifton Road, late 19th early
20th Century.
I did well at school and I was generally top. I was in Standard Seven for three years and that was as high as standards went in those days. For 12 months I was sent into the teachers' private room to teach the dunces. Those were the days. We were taught the three R's in classes of over 40 pupils.
Annie Farrington (née Bickerstaff)

Prizes And The Wooden Spoon.
One year I won a prize in a competition for an essay about a film I had seen. It was a large book called "The Arctic and its conditions" and I also won a book of tokens to take to the picture house on top of Bredon Hill. The year I left I wrote a play about the Christmas Pudding, which we performed with each child holding a placard which said which ingredient they were, such as fruit or sugar. Then I had to "mix" them all up with a wooden spoon.
Winifred Berkeley

High School Science Congress.
Nairobi, Kenya, 1990's.
In my time at high school I was lucky enough to win a prize at the national schools innovative design awards. Schools took part in the annual 'Science Congress' competition, and my effort one year was an environmentally friendly system (ahead of my time?). It consisted of wrapping copper pipes around traditional large cooking pots, so that as cooking took place water in the pipes was heated.
Rizwan Janmohamed

Points Mean Prizes.
Bishop Challoner, 1950's.
The school was split into four houses. This system made us competitive and being late for school lost points. Being reproached by your own house colleagues made you feel worse than having the cane although we usually got that too.
Reginald Arthur Brown

A Trier.
Yardley, 1990's.
In end of year presentations in the assembly hall, we would be called out individually to receive certificates representing our achievements. For me an award for punctuality and attendance was a given. 'Good effort' was it seemed to me an ever present note on my certificates whatever the subject.
Sabreena Ali

Scholarship.
I got straight "A"s and I got a really nice gift, a scholarship to go to Iran to study the Persian language. So I had a really nice summer after my A Levels.
Sukaina Khimji

Plotting The Inspection.
Ghana, Africa, 1970's and 80's.
Once a month, there was an inspection of the school premises by a team from the school staff. Included in this inspection were 'plots', areas of the school grounds allocated to each pupil. Once allocated to us we were personally responsible for maintaining and keeping 'our' plot clean and tidy. The inspection was usually on a Saturday morning. We would have to stand by our plot while the inspection was carried out. It was possible, during the school week, to be called from our classes to the plot if anything was found amiss with it. We pupils were members of a school house which we could earn points for. It gave us great motivation as the house with the most points would win a trophy and a prize.
Peter Owusu

Teacher's Pet.
I was a class prefect at one time, helping to keep order, run errands etc. I didn't think much of the role since it invited being called 'Teacher's Pet' by the other kids.
Pat Johnson (née Shine)

Perfect Prefect.

Dennis Road School, 1950's.

I was proud to be the prefect in Mr Tebbit's class, especially as I was elected by my class mates. All the pupils in 4.1 had to vote. There is a theory though, still pondered on by myself even today; it is that I was elected because I was a very easy going chap, friendly to all, and a pushover.

Maurice Arthur Evans

Prefect Power.

Kenya.

I had to tell off a bunch of teenage boys for misbehaving and I thought that was really funny because they were a lot taller than me and I had to scream and shout at them.

Sukaina Khimji

HIGH DAYS AND HOLIDAYS

Assemblies

On Reflection.

Each day at Clifton Road would begin with morning prayers. Mrs Formby would stand with her back to us facing a picture of Jesus knocking on a door. She always knew if we misbehaved during these prayers. It was quite a while before I discovered that she used the glass of the picture as a mirror.

Peter Davis

Over Our Heads.

Heathmount held assemblies daily, which were always lively. We'd sing songs such as "If I had a Hammer" and "Morning Glory" the lyrics of the song coming up on an overhead projector and accompanied by Mrs Salway on the piano. At the end of the month, usually on a Friday, parents were invited to the assemblies and the merit awards would be announced.

Nazreen Bi

Golden Times.

Wallasey High School, late 50's and early 60's.

The daily assemblies were impressive, held in the Hall lined with honours boards lettered in gold. There we sat awaiting a signal, when a door would open from the sixth form room and a line of prefects would emerge, heads held high as they walked proudly to sit in their row. How we admired them, with their shapely figures and pleated skirts.

These assemblies were memorable with rousing hymns and readings; hymns such as, "Let us now praise famous men" and Blake's "Jerusalem", and passages from The Apocrypha. Wonderful, meaningful times – not as imaginative as assemblies in schools are today, but stirring and never to be forgotten.
Wendy Beynon (née Forsyth)

Loss of faith!
Some of us boys changed our religion – in school only – for the very purpose of getting out of assemblies. Generally the tone of the school assembly was set by C of E traditions, so if you were of another denomination you were excused assembly. Several of us became 'Catholics' and were ushered in to a separate room where we could discuss anything that interested us – what was on the telly the night before, or the latest sports news etc. Sometime we were sat down on the balcony of the hall during assembly, which meant very much we didn't have to listen to what was going on or indeed take part.
Chris Sutton

Band Time.
Pakistan.
Assembly was always outside because it was so hot and after that we had a band play. We used to do exercises to the band every morning.
Naseem Somani

Dying To Take Part.
I played Jesus in a play once. I had to walk around the hall and get crucified on the wall bars. It was very nerve racking. I forgot my lines and there was another girl helping me with my lines.
Bob Dearing

Happiest Days.
Rushcliffe, Nottingham.
One year the school put on a play, probably a nativity effort, as I remember the characters of Mary and Joseph being on stage. I had been practising my part for weeks leading up to the event. On the night it seemed so splendid to me, bright lights, the stage, colourful scenery, costumes, and my mum in the audience.

A Christmas party remains in the memory too. We were all dressed up, dancing with joined hands and moving in a circle, spinning like mad people and singing to a Mariah Carey recording of "All I Want for Christmas is You."
Selina Brown

Me And My Axe.

A memory from my early days at school was appearing as one of the seven dwarfs in a Christmas production of Snow White and the Seven Dwarfs and struggling to carry over my shoulder a full size long handled axe – something that would not be allowed today. The only line I had to say was "We're right behind you".

Alan Hemming

Festivities Singer By Default.
Perry Beeches.

I became a singer as a result of messing about talking and laughing with my friends in assembly. We were told to stand to one side and were later joined by others who had not behaved themselves in the playground and elsewhere. We were lined up and told to sing; as a result I was selected to sing at the Harvest Festival. As a result of that I was selected to play a part in a school musical written by one of the teachers. It was well received and there was talk of a recording.

Peter Cole

Holy Mary.
Clifton Road.

Because I was quite tall they used to pick me for the Nativity but I used to just sit there. I remember doing it for a number of years and I was always Mary. It was scary so I didn't do anything like rock the baby. I used to sit there with something white, possibly a tea towel, on my head. I think I just looked holy. There were no lines to say, just singing. They may have been trying to encourage me out of my shyness.

Victoria Jeffs

This Gnome Got Sacked.

I was in a play in the last year at school as one of Father Christmas's gnomes. I remember my costume was a hat made out of a paper potato sack painted green and ruffled up.

Jo Lea

Brave Dressing For The School Play.

One year the school put on Hiawatha and I was to play an Indian Brave. I was reluctant to ask my mum to make

Going Dutch in 1937 at Mary Street Junior School, Balsall Heath, Birmingham.

the outfit I needed as she was mother to seven of us and very busy, so I had a go at it myself. I cut up two pillow cases and made them into a form of britches. Finding some red material about two inches wide – possibly my sister's ribbons – I sewed it onto the britches as stripes, with the longest, loosest stitches you have ever seen.
Michael Henry Fitzpatrick

The Sickly Angel.
Bristol, 1960's.
In year six we had a nativity play which was performed in the local church. Along with other girls I was selected as an Angel. During the play we were to hide behind the church altar and come out on cue and 'appear' to the central characters and audience. On the day of the performance I felt ill all day at school. Getting home, I poured myself a glass of orange squash and was so sick I had to run to the toilet. I missed out on being an Angel.
Marion Ridsdill

Royalty At School.
Glebe Farm Park, Stechford.
As I was a very diminutive girl I always got the part of a page-boy. Every year our plays seemed to feature royalty; Kings and Queens, castles and page-boys.
Gladys Ford (née Woolley)

Mirroring Life.
Springfield J. and I, 1960's.
I played the magic mirror in the production of Snow White and the Seven Dwarfs. I had a big cardboard costume – a frame with silver foil and my head sticking through as well as itchy gold tights.
Tracy Doherty

A performance of Proserpine at Tindal St Infants' School, Balsall Heath, Birmingham. 1931.

CELEBRATIONS AND PARTIES

Hurt In The Dragon.
Sparkbrook, 1980's.
With its multicultural ethos the school celebrated a mix of cultures with plays or parades. On one occasion we put together a Chinese dragon to celebrate the Chinese

New Year. I was inside the dragon with other kids giving it life and movement, when suddenly the kid in front of me stopped. I crashed into him hurting my face. I was not happy at the time, but I still carried on with my part in the display.
Sabreena Ali

Rule Britannia!
Empire Day at Clifton School in
the 1900's.
Empire Day was quite an event. Everyone dressed in costumes of Commonwealth countries and the Head Girl would be Britannia. This was the only time we had our photographs taken.
Mrs Osborne

Boys Will Be Girls.
I think there was a time when some of the teachers dressed up as the Spice Girls, which was fun because they were men! It was the funniest thing.
Dalal Olewa

Alice Young as Britannia at Empire Day, Clifton Road School, Balsall Heath, Birmingham. 1917.

The May Queen.
One of my friends at Upper Highgate School was a girl named Elsie. At least I thought she was my friend until one day in May. We were rehearsing for the May Day celebrations and the crowning of the May Queen. Most of the class had a part. They played fairies, flowers and birds. I was a fairy. Miss Bowman had to go out of the room and she left Elsie in charge of the class. Elsie became power-mad and I was one of the first to be called out for talking. She reported me to Miss Bowman when she came back and alas I was a fairy no more! That was my punishment and Elsie wore a self-satisfied look for the rest of the day. I was too young for it to bother me but I did have the last laugh because I was chosen to play the May Queen. Poor Elsie must have hated me but I bore no malice. I enjoyed my role as May Queen. I was heralded by a blackbird who had to whistle for me to appear. This part was played by a boy named Horace, who whistled beautifully. Other pupils danced around the Maypole which was fixed in the middle of the hall.
Nell Wilkins

The Coronation In Colour.
Clifton Road.

In 1953 to celebrate the Coronation the whole school marched to the Imperial Cinema on the Moseley Road to see a Technicolor film of the event. Remember a lot of people didn't have a television in those days and nobody had a colour one. It was all black and white. I was a bit bored by it though. I was only six and I'd have preferred Cowboys and Indians!
Graham Pearson

The Coronation in Essex.

I was at school at the time of the Coronation in 1953 and a most tremendous fuss was made of it all. By chance we were doing a project on Princess Elizabeth's trip to Africa. We were dutifully assembling scrapbooks of newspaper cuttings when her father, the king, died and she rushed back home so we already had a good start on the whole thing. I made an embroidered sampler to commemorate the Coronation, which took me ages. We were also all given a very small bar of chocolate in a special commemorative tin, which I still have.
Val Hart (née Cooper)

Teachers' Day.
Madhya Pradesh, India.

We used to celebrate "Teachers' Day" at our school on the 5th September each year when the children would stage a play for the teachers, decorate the classroom and bring in cakes. We would wear our own clothes instead of uniform and the teachers would give us sweets.
Nisha Sharma

Sampler for the Coronation of Queen Elizabeth sewn by Val Hart (née Cooper) at primary school. 1953.

School Discos.

We had school discos on Friday lunchtimes in the hall. The music was predominately reggae round about that time. They had all these dances where you used to have to stand in a line and all the girls did the same motions. The boys used

to do all the jumping up and down, not body popping but a version of that before it became popular.
Kerry Smith

TRIPS

A Day Out With The Gentry.

Every summer Lord and Lady Longford invited the school to attend Tullynally Castle for a day of sports and fun. We would have egg and spoon races, three legged races, croquet etc. Swings, slides and various types of equipment were erected in the grounds for our entertainment. In the afternoon we would sit down to tea in a big marquee on the lawn and were waited on by the castle staff. At the end of the day we went into the castle and there in the hall Lord and Lady Longford would stand behind a long table laden with all sorts of games and toys and they would present us with the gift of our choice. We came away feeling very happy and the sun always shone on the day we went to the castle.
Valerie Ganderton

New Broughton School, Wrexham on a visit to Buckingham Palace. 1950's.

Royal Visit And A Victorian Event.

There was a royal visit to Birmingham in the late 80's. Two children from each class were selected to make up a group of children to attend the visit to Birmingham city centre. To us young ones this seemed so far away as to be in another town. I remember we waved flags at the royal car, but I can't remember who was inside, the Queen or Prince Charles.

One Saturday a number of pupils travelled to Highbury Hall where we enacted the Victorian classroom. We girls dressed in pinafores and wore ribbon in our hair. The boys wore jackets and clothes as they would have in Victorian times. We sang songs and played games which involved picking straws, which told you what prize you had won.

Nazreen Bi

Bread Taken From My Mother's Mouth.

We were taken on a number of school trips from Perry Beeches. An incident on one trip lives long in the memory. We went to Boulogne in France. I remember having difficulty buying a pen as what French I knew deserted me. And then there was the trip home; I had bought a baguette with the idea that my mother could taste some French bread. It didn't make the trip. I fell asleep and my fellow class mates couldn't resist the smell. Only a crust remained when I woke up.

Peter Cole

Tripping Along In Tap Shoes.
Audley Road.

We were often taken to the Ideal Home Exhibition, also to the seaside – Rhyl, New Brighton and Liverpool across the Mersey for instance. I remember one trip, that in order to go, I badly needed a new pair of shoes. My family, with ten children, could not afford them. When the school heard, I was called to the headmaster's office and told to look in a large box of shoes, all donated to the school, and find a pair to fit me. I found a pair of tap-dancing shoes which were white with cracked uppers. I took them home and painted them black. The head couldn't believe it when he saw them on my feet.

Gladys Ford (née Woolley)

Lost.

We went on a trip to Wales for five days. Next to the camp was a forest which we were forbidden to explore. One night we snuck over the fence and hid. All the teachers and people in the camp were searching for us. They even phoned the police.

Helen Donaghy

In The Outback.
Australia.
School trips had both educational and social elements in that they tended to be outdoor pursuits. The school bus was used for these trips which might be for a day or a week long camp for rock-climbing and exploring the outback. One trip, where we were 200 km into a planned 600 km outward journey, saw the rear window fall out of the bus. We spent the rest of the trip without the rear window or with people holding it in place whenever necessary.
Deborah Simpson (née Style)

That Sinking Feeling.
I remember a trip to the Malverns. It was a wet day, so the school party went to the Winter Gardens. The rain eventually stopped and we found a small boating pool. A number of us had a ride in a boat and when we came back in we had to step off the boat on to the shore. I missed my step and landed in yellowy-green water. It flashed through my mind that I should try to remember all the things I had been taught about swimming. My knees touched down on the bottom of the pool and I realised it wasn't that deep. Soaked through I was taken into the backroom of a teashop. I was stripped off, including my knickers and given a lady's coat to wear while my clothes dried. When I got home my mother wondered at my dishevelled state, but laughed her head off when I told her what happened.
Anon

IN THE PLAYGROUND

Kiss Chase.
There was kiss chase. You had to run away and the person who was caught had to kiss someone. I don't know if this was a punishment or a reward, this kiss!

We also used to do "On the Good Ship Alley-o" and "Oranges and Lemons." We used to skip and everyone took turns at turning this big rope.
Victoria Jeffs

Let The Sparks Fly.
After school the playground became our own with no other children around and many competitive games took place before we were ushered out by the caretaker and we headed home. I remember a lad coming into school who wore enormous boots with shiny steel toecaps and the soles studded with rows of steel studs. When he ran the sparks flew and no-one ventured near when he had the ball, although because we always played with a tennis ball it nearly always got lost between those

enormous boots. We lost numerous balls in the adjoining gardens and despite repeated warnings from the headmaster about climbing over the fences someone usually managed to retrieve them or find another ball from somewhere and the games continued.

Alan Hemming

Dipping.

In order to decide who 'it' was in the game of tag, we performed something called the dipping game. We stood in a circle and put a fist or a foot forward. Using a rhyme ("Eeny, meeny, miney mo…"), one by one we would 'fall out' of the circle. The girl left in at the end was 'it'.

Joyce Ashworth

Superior Girls.

The buildings occupied by the senior section of St Thomas's were two storeys as opposed to the Infants and Juniors which were single. At playtime the senior girls

Not all fun and games in the playground.

used an upper floor playground while the boys were below on ground level. This separation was not something used in the classrooms. In fact the general rule was that a girl would not be seated with another girl, with the same applied to the boys. It was obviously thought that there was less chance of mischief with a girl/boy arrangement.
Pat Johnson (née Shine)

Rock It.
Mico Practising School, Jamaica, 1962–5.
We girls played lots of skipping games during breaks and other games too. In one we sat down in a circle, each of us having a rock in our hand and we tapped it on the ground rhythmically, in accompaniment to words we were reciting. At a given point in the recital we placed the rock we were holding in front of the girl next to us. We picked up the new rock and did it all over again.
Marcia Vizor

How To Play Marbles And Win.
We made a lot of use of the playground, as we got away from the school dinners as soon as possible. I hated them. They were vile, some sort of gruel that they served up. When in the playground, we played marbles for long periods of the school year. I remember that I cheated a lot. The alternative for us boys was football.
John Bealt

Cut Knees.
The playground at the junior school was a bit rough. You would always get a bit frightened of getting knocked over as you'd finish up with cut knees or elbows.
Barbara Rainbird

Piggy Back Fights.
At break times we would piggy back fight. You would have another kid on your back and they used to stick their legs out like battering rams and see who would fall off first. It was good fun.
Jim Atkinson

The Hopscotch League.
We played the usual playground games you would expect, the girls doing the skipping, reciting games, and handstands, while we boys would pursue football and marbles etc. One game crossed over the demarcation line between us, that of

Fun and games in the playground. 1940's.

hopscotch. We boys invented a league of hopscotch with three hopscotch pitches; the second was bigger than the first and the third bigger than the second. We had to progress from pitch 1 to 3 by promotion. We had to get a regular high score on pitch 1 before being promoted to pitch 2. That was as far as I got – pitch 2.
Mark Houldcroft

Boys' Games.
In the playground at my junior school we entertained ourselves with various games and pastimes. Tag is the game where one person is 'on' or 'it' and has to touch or 'tag' another person to make them 'it'. A hut built at one end of the playground was our location for the game. We ran around this structure tagging and being tagged. The entrance to the hut and the fire doors on the opposite side were sanctuaries where you couldn't be tagged.

We boys also played Jets. In this one we ran around the playground with our arms held out and backwards like jet aircraft wings, making jet engine noises and counting down from 10, slowing down our speed with the count. Being bumped into by another Jet, started up our engines again.

Conkers was popular too, the game where you threaded a shiny and hard horse chestnut on to a piece of string which was swung at your rival's conker, also on string, trying to break it. Success by one or the other left the winner with a champion conker. We boys tried several techniques with which to harden our conkers such as soaking them in vinegar; I don't think any of them ever worked.
Peter Cole

Fingers And Thumbs.

Playtimes were fun. Sometimes it was cold and we didn't have gloves so we used to wear our dads' or brothers' socks on our hands. They were thick socks and we never used to have any thumbs!

I loved football, skipping games and Chinese skipping. We didn't have an elastic band so we used to use our mums' stockings. We tied them together and put them around our feet.

Pam Mullin

Whatever The Weather.

We were always outside whatever the weather for playtime. We amused ourselves with lots of games, Ring-a-Ring-a-Roses, The Farmer's In His Den, different skipping games and a game in which we used hundreds, if not thousands, of elastic bands joined together. We bought them by the packet to form an endless band which was stretched around the legs of two girls facing each other. Starting at the ankles we moved the elastic higher and higher as we danced over and around it. Another game had us clapping our hands to a beat and reciting the lyrics of a pop song that was in the charts at the time, which began something like; "My mother told me, not to kiss a soldier; my mother told me..............."

Marion Ridsdill

Hopscotch And The Elastic Band. 1980's and 90's.

The school day was from 9am till 3.30pm with lunch time 12 noon till 1pm. In the playground we would draw hopscotch pitches with boxes numbered 1 to 10,

then shout "One foot," "Two foot" as we progressed on the pitch. A new skipping game came along just before I left primary, circa 1997, which involved the use of a large elastic band. Two girls faced each other a distance apart with the band stretching round the backs of their legs and at a determined height from the ground. Up to three other girls would stand alongside the band jumping in and out with an accompanying rhyme, "Indoors, outdoors, indoors, outdoors."
Sabreena Ali

Heroes.
We would play a lot of what we saw on TV like Man from Uncle, Thunderbirds, and Captain Scarlet.
Jo Lea

Jacks.
Essex And Lincolnshire, 1970's and 80's.
In the junior school playground, we skipped to "Brown Girl in the Ring" and other rhymes; we used hula-hoops, played on hopscotch pitches and sat in a circle playing Jacks. The player 'on', or to go first, was decided by the number of jacks, (steel, plastic star shapes or stones), caught on the back of the hand. She or he tossed up a ball and while it was still in the air, picked up one of five jacks lying on the ground. After catching the ball with the same hand, the retrieved jack was passed to the other hand. The action was repeated until all the jacks had been picked up. The game got more complex as it progressed.
Patsy Stewart

Airflow.
We used to play football with plastic airflow balls. They used to cost about 10p. The trouble was they used to get cracked easily and then they were no good so we had to buy a new one.
Steve Sutton

Meadows Primary School.
For those of us who lived near the school, the school caretaker a Mr Woodridge, left the school gates open so we could use the playground for a game of football. We were there for hours at a time, playing until it was so dark you couldn't see the ball. Mr Woodridge would have to come out to us on the longer evenings to say, "Look kids I've got to lock-up."
Chris Sutton

Break time in the playground.

Football.

I always played football every break time, which I really enjoyed. We just ran around the playground.

Scott Hosker

No Football.

Playtimes were the best. We used to really play up the boys and take the football off them and run. Things like that, we did have fun.

Neelam Rose

What No Games?

I was a bit surprised when I got to High School, I thought everyone was going to be running around the playground. Obviously people wouldn't be doing that, they were gossiping and standing in groups. I wasn't used to that because I used to play football with the boys in primary school. I didn't like that at all, but I had to adjust.

Nowrah Abdul

The Great Outdoors, Budapest.

There were acres of room for us to play and exercise, and we were chucked out of the buildings whatever the weather. There were huge gardens which I thought were wonderful. There was a large football pitch and tennis courts, which were used for physical education, and that we were allowed to use after school. This is where we would have a smoke on our cheap Hungarian cigarettes.
Laura Szendy

SCHOOL MEALS AND CHOCOLATE CONCRETE

The Soup Run.
Clifton Road, 1920's.

So many lads here had fathers who were out of work and with big families so there was a lot of hardship. One of the teachers used to bring in a loaf of bread for them. They also had tickets for free dinners but they had to run down to Sherbourne Road School at lunch time to get their bowl of soup.
Jack Billington

Identification Of The Poorest.

If you were identified as needy by the welfare people, you were entitled to free school meals and vouchers for footwear and clothing. The ticket for the free dinner was a different colour to those that had to be paid for, and the free boots handed out at the Evening Mail premises were clearly stamped 'Daily Mail'.
Maurice Arthur Evans

PRACTICE.

Six girls cooking.

Breakfast On The Move.
1930's.

We'd call for Charlie Davies every morning on the way to school. Charlie's Dad was a foreman metal spinner at Fisher and Ludlow's factory in Bradford Street. He was very well-paid and had bacon for breakfast every morning, cooked by his wife. She'd always give us each a slice of white bread dipped in the bacon fat. It was delicious.

Bernard Jackson

Greasy Water And Stale Bread, Lunch For Poor Children.
1930's.

You had to have a ticket to get school meals at Mary Street School. The poorer children were given soup and bread which they said tasted like 'greasy water and stale bread'. Most people were poor then.

Bernard Jackson.

The Christmas Party.
Loxton Street Juniors, Nechells,
1940's and 50's.

I stayed at school for dinner and remember that the dinner period regime was very strict; you had to eat every thing you were given or took for yourself. Mostly this was all right but I did hate rhubarb crumble, though I like it now. The Christmas party was so different when it came to food. We loved the trifle and jelly served up on those long festively dressed benches placed together in long lines.

Dennis Hammond

School Meals.
Wallasey High School.

We sat at tables for nine; four on each side and one at the end who had the task of serving the bowls of food to the rest of the table. Blue plastic lacy doilies were used as place mats, a ladylike touch in those days.

Christmas Party at Heath Mount School, Balsall Heath, Birmingham. 1980's.

One class was designated to stand in the middle of the canteen and wait to be sent to fill up spaces. We hated doing this – you had to eat with girls unknown to you, or worse, a lot older. When the canteen became too noisy a bell was rung and we were made to finish our meals in total silence. You could go to the hatch for seconds – more gravy and mashed potato or lumpy custard – but I enjoyed it all! There were not the choices of today; the meal was set and we ate it hungrily. Chocolate Crunch, or the aptly named Fly Cemetery were popular.

Wendy Beynon (née Forsyth)

Fond Memories Of "Concrete".
Due to lack of space at Moseley C of E School, the meals service soon moved to larger premises in the Church Hall on the corner of School Road/Oxford Road, the site of the present school. I stayed for meals for a short time but then reverted to going home for lunch. However, I still fondly remember the sponge pudding and 'chocolate concrete' that used to come down to the school in time for distribution at afternoon break.

Alan Hemming

Village Soup.
At my school in Wythall there weren't any school dinners provided but then a teacher arrived who had the bright idea of making soup. So I found myself standing to scrape carrots and other vegetables outside by the pump. We cooked it up on the top of the classroom stove.

Betty Thornicroft

School Dinners And Frog Spawn At St Thomas C. of E.
Although we didn't live that far from school at Upper Gough Street, at first I stopped for school dinners because my mother was working so there was no one at home. It wasn't long before I began to hate the meals they served up. The meat was always tough and the cabbage barely palatable but we were

A struggle with the pudding.

forced to eat it as well as the sweet known as semolina, made from the hard residue of flour after milling, which had the character of frog spawn. Later my father came home to cook our dinner, but that ended too when I got old enough to rebel.
Pat Johnson (née Shine)

Lovely School Dinners.
Lucerne, Wyoming.
School lunches were subsidised. The menu included Hot Dogs on a plate, Spaghetti Bolognaise and toasted cheese sandwiches which we kids especially liked. I was happy to stay at school for lunch even though my Lucerne home was only a quarter of a mile away.
Ron Vannelli

Walking To My Dinner.
St. Johns RC School, Mary Street, 1940's and 50's.
Those of us that stopped for school dinner had to walk about three-quarters of a mile to the meal facility. Whatever the weather, come rain, come snow, we walked all the way down George Street from the annex at the top, across Edward Road into Wenman Street, to a building on the right opposite Hallam Street. The dinners always consisted basically of boiled carrots and cabbage. The sweets were awful or should that be 'the' sweet was awful – terrible. You were not allowed to

In the playground after lunch, at Clifton Infants' School, Balsall Heath, Birmingham, 2000.

throw anything away, if you took it, you had to eat it. And then we had to walk back to school. I was frozen so many times.
Reginald Arthur Brown

Eat Up.
The general attitude from both home and school was that you had to eat everything you were given. This was fine if it was stodgy puddings which I loved, but not so good for lots of other items: deadly hard liver, grey mashed potato with lumps, orangey-pink tapioca with uncooked dry lumps, semolina with globular lumps.... The most popular children were those who liked it all and ate everyone else's for them.
Anita Halliday

Eat Everything, Everyone.
Clifton Road, 1950's.
The dinners were pretty grim and the rule was that you had to eat everything you were given, with no choice of menu. If you left anything the remark always was, "How dare you? There are people starving in the world." No one could go out to play until everyone had eaten everything, so if it was sago the dishes got swapped around.
Graham Pearson

What A Waste.
I was having school lunch and they were cutting down on waste. You used to have to clear away your waste and I had left a bit of custard. There was Miss C by the waste bins inspecting everyone's plates and leftover morsels and she made me go back and finish my custard.
Steve Sutton

Shattering.
One thing I didn't like for school dinners was liver, but you were told you had got to eat it because it was good for your blood. I used to love the chocolate concrete. You put your spoon in and it shattered.
Dawn McGhie

Dangerous Walk, Better Dinner.
Albert Bradbeer Primary School.
The school meals weren't good. A dinner lady stood over me while I ate lumpy rice pudding with raisins. Forced to eat what was making me heave, I resolved to start going home for dinner. This led to a dangerous walk home along the busy Longbridge Lane, where the Austin motor works added to the traffic. My mother

came to meet me at a halfway point. The time taken to get home and back to school left me with just enough time to get my dinner down. One day the yard gate had been left off the catch and my dog got out and followed me. He was run over and killed.

Sally Williams (née Hall)

Dinner Dealings.
Highgate, 1960's and 70's.
We were given money for school dinners which we didn't always use to buy dinners, pocketing the cash. Or we might be given a ticket for a dinner which we would trade for money. The buyer would get a cheaper meal and the seller gained too. Not having to go into the dining hall meant we had more time to go to the park at lunch time.

One of the gang had an uncle in the restaurant business. He worked in one of the two Indian restaurants established on the Moseley Road and we would sometimes go there to eat at dinner time. One was called Shareen Kadah (House of Taste); it was not a smart place at the time, with cracked mats on the tables, but it was what we kids wanted to do.

Mark Houldcroft

Lovely Desserts.
Handsworth, 1970's.
I loved the school dinners; especially when from the third year we were allowed chips with our meals. The puddings were great too, ginger squares, chocolate sponge with custard, and upside-down pineapple.

Samantha Hines

Beetroot With Everything.
Clifton Road.
I hated school dinners. There always seemed to be beetroot on them, not pickled but cooked and diced, it tasted horrid. The puddings were nice though; jam tart and custard, chocolate sponge and peppermint sauce, mmmmmm.

Sheila Reynolds (née Moore)

Smash!
At primary school they used to give us what we called "smash potato". They used to give us dry potatoes – it wasn't pleasant. If they were handing it out at lunch I would dread it. We used to get boiled cabbage and liver too. I don't think there was much choice.

Bob Dearing

Lumpy Custard.

At my primary school the school meals were horrible. There was no taste to them and the custard was always lumpy.

Scott Hosker

Dinner Or Cigarettes.
Tudor Grange Secondary, 1980's.

There was a set meal, usually that was a choice between two main courses, perhaps a sausage with an alternative taken with salad or chips. I quite liked the dinners on the whole and loved the chips. They were beautifully soggy. This changed as the school brought in more variety. For instance I remember pizza coming on to the menu. As I got older I ate less but smoked more. My dinner money became pocket money spent on cigarettes.

Neil Monroe

Mum Knows Best.
Perry Beeches.

I had not, up to this point, stayed for school dinners because of the proximity of home to school. But as I moved up to juniors the Headmaster, Mr. Cummins, thought that it was important for his pupils to have a good meal and promoted school dinners. The fact that I wanted to take sandwiches to eat at school had to be backed up by my mother, and we had to see him together to confirm it. Even so he was not satisfied. He tried to convince my mother that he and the school could feed me better than her. She said no, she would feed me herself. I never went to school dinners.

Peter Cole

Peter Cole, ready for the school photograph.

Next.......!

Primary school meals were quite pleasant. They used to give us a milk carton, which I loved drinking from. I used to like the food. Secondary school was like a chicken factory, and mealtimes were just a process.

Razia Khatun

It Makes A Change.

I used to love eating all the English food because at home my mother only made Indian food. I used to love eating all the mashed potatoes, carrots and peas that the white children didn't like.

At Middle School I briefly had sandwiches, but my mother used to embarrass me because she put Indian food in my lunchbox.
Iram Weir

Adjustments.

My parents cooked Caribbean food. At school the food was different but we adjusted. The one thing I couldn't adjust to was the bottle of milk. I refused to drink it because I just didn't like milk. They made me drink it sometimes, but I did struggle. It made me ill.
Yvette John

Doughnut Dinners.
Nottingham, 1990's.

I admit I liked school dinners. I remember being the last to finish eating. I'm not sure if that was because I was slow or because we had to sit and wait our turn as a class. We were called up by the grade we were in. I was one of the few who actually liked lumpy custard. The group of girls I sat with often had a competition when eating doughnuts. The test was not to lick your lips when eating this sugar coated sweet. The first girl to do so lost.
Selina Brown

Spaghetti For Once.
The Open Air School, Birmingham.

We had all our meals there, breakfast, dinner, tea before we came away. We had spaghetti one day and nobody would eat it, so the headmistress said, "Well you will all sit there till you do and there will be no pudding for anybody". Believe me we all sat there and ate it. Mind you, they never ever served up it up again.
Olive Dowdeswell (née Rose)

Food, Glorious Food.

Feeding Pop Stars.
St Luke's 1960's and 70's.

I was in the kitchen at St. Luke's. We made chocolate concrete, steak and kidney pudding, currant puddings and rhubarb. We put olives in some of the stuff and none of the kids would eat olives. Both of the Campbells from UB40 went to St Luke's School. I used to give them their dinners.

Gwen White

Halal.

Coming from a country where everything was Halal we found it difficult to understand that things were different. We knew we couldn't eat pork but at school we didn't grasp the concept and used to eat turkey drumsticks and burgers. We'd come across the concept of Halal, but we were too young to understand.

Shahida Aslam

Enjoyable School Meals!
Early 1980's.

Many years ago I was a pupil of Highgate Comprehensive. My first year was spent at Highgate Annexe, which is the old Art School on Moseley Road, opposite the Moseley Road Baths. At break time it was straight to the Tuck Shop and when the hand held bell was rung for dinner we would run to the main block. An orderly queue was formed to receive lunch on the production of a green-coloured 'dinner ticket' similar to a raffle ticket. The words Birmingham City Council were printed on one side and on the other Non Transferable.

Our meals were enjoyable, served on a sturdy plastic compartment plate so that the dinner ladies placed the grub in the right places. The meals ranged from pork pie to fish fingers with a range of vegetables, not forgetting the two scoops of special mash served using the ice cream scooper. Puddings ranged from apple pie and custard to chocolate concrete cake, a firm favourite for many.

Tesh Champaneri

Popular Pizza.
King Edward's Camp Hill, 1990's.

I told my mum that I had lots of vegetables and fruit but I was always having the pizzas, burgers and chips!

Naveed Somani

Variety, please.

In my primary school we didn't get much choice and there wasn't a lot of variety at all. At secondary school the meals were good and fairly healthy. There was variety and we could comment on what types of food we wanted.

Sameera Bi

English Food For A Change.

I come from an Asian background so I used to get bored of the same things, like rice and curry every day so I was excited when I had my dinners at school. You got spaghetti and mashed potato which I absolutely loved. They were the best thing about school.

Sheikh Amina Khanam

Meals On Wheels.

Surprisingly we did have school dinners. They arrived at the school in insulated containers, but by the time the desks were put together and the meal organised it was invariably lukewarm. The potatoes and vegetables were usually edible, but the meat! When the teachers weren't looking we would throw lumps of it on top of the corner cupboard. I guess the mice had quite a feast.

Peter Davis

Milk Lollies.

One day the milk was frozen solid in the cartons and so they put them on the radiators to thaw them out.

Chris Sutton

Extra, Please.
St. George's Road Primary School, Wallasey.

We were tough. Perhaps it was due to post war plain food and little bottles of milk with straws at morning break which were brought round by the milk monitor. Sometimes there were bottles left over and you could have an extra one, but not so nice if they had been left until afternoon in a warm classroom.

Wendy Beynon (née Forsyth)

Milk Monitor.

I was the milk monitor, which meant that we put straws in the milk for everyone, which was an important job at the time.

Barbara Rainbird

Drink Up.

On the bad side, one teacher shouted at us about drinking up our free milk which was often warm and horrible to drink. To get the milk down I would hold my nose while drinking it.

Samantha Hines

School Milk and More.
Sparkbrook, 1980's.

I think we may have had to pay for school milk in the 80's, probably 10 pence for a carton, not a bottle. Some days it could get warm after being left out in the weather. This never prevented me from enjoying it, as it came with a biscuit at story time.

Sabreena Ali

Chapter 5

Changes

It's fascinating to find in these memories of school a reflection of what else was happening at the time. The most striking examples of this are the memories of going to school during the Second World War. Some pupils were evacuated but all had to make major adjustments to a different way of life.

In contrast, later changes seem less important although they had an effect on those who remembered them, especially the Teachers' Strike and the move to GCSEs.

SECOND WORLD WAR

A class at Tindal Street School, Balsall Heath, Birmingham. 1939.

School Bombed.
Tindal Street, 1941.
We arrived one morning to find part of the building fronting Cromer Road destroyed by an overnight raid. This was early in 1941 and I recall a group of us being marched down to Mary Street School to view our new school and we were registered to start at the school on the 17th February 1941. During all this time I can't remember ever carrying a gas mask although photographs from the period always seem to show school children carrying them. Although the sounds and sights from this period are still quite vivid I can't recall being in fear or frightened.
Alan Hemming

Taking Shelter.
We sometimes went to school having spent most of the night in the Anderson shelter in our garden. I think I was too young to realise the gravity of the situation. I used to enjoy going into the shelter, as we had a double-sized one which we

Bomb Damage at Mary Street School, Balsall Heath, Birmingham. Early 1940's.

shared with my Aunt and cousins who lived two doors away. My uncle was in the army, and my father was working away in Coalville in a munitions factory.
Anne Hemming

Shelter Or Smoke.
Dennis Road and Moseley Road Art School.
I went to Dennis Road School which closed at the beginning of the war for about a year. Eventually it was sorted out that a teacher came round to someone's house once a week for a couple of hours. That was all the education we got at that time. Later during the war I went to Moseley Road Art School. I remember we turned up for school one morning and found that the Methodist Church at the top of Lime Grove had disappeared into a pile of rubble. After that they built us a surface brick air raid shelter on top of the rubble. Then, if there was an air raid, a crocodile of pupils ran across the rubble to the main shelter in the annex (the old school building in Lime Grove). However, some of us were very naughty and used to detach ourselves from the rest and nip into the brick shelter to have a smoke, rejoining the crocodile when it came back.
Maurice Cleaver

Fiction Or Fiction?
Clifton Road.
There was a spire on the junior section of the school and it had a red line running down the slates and the story was that it was the blood of a German paratrooper.
Victoria Jeffs

Lessons At Home.
Clifton Road.
When the war started the school closed because it was an ARP First Aid centre. When the school was evacuated I stayed at home and we didn't have any school for about six months. After that time the teachers used to come round to a house, say the front room, and six or seven children from that area would get lessons about three times a week.
Len Powell

Take Shelter.
Francis Road.
I can remember being in the nursery in Francis Road and some German aircraft coming over. They ran us all down into some shelters.
Carol Woolley

It's Beetroot Juice Not Blood.
Wythall and Camp Hill.

I went to the village school in Wythall until I was eleven. One day during the war we came out of school and were standing around chatting when a German plane came over and dive bombed, shooting at us. I was terrified and ran home. We didn't have an air raid shelter so mother was hiding in the pantry. I dashed in and knocked into her with the result that I finished up with beetroot all over me.

Later during the war I went to Camp Hill Grammar School and remember looking across the road to the railway lines where Italian Prisoners of War were working. They wore brown uniforms with a big circular yellow patch. They were billeted at Swanshurst Park where the Fire Station is now.
Betty Thornicroft

Talking To Prisoners.
Wyoming, USA.

I remember seeing German prisoners of war working in the beet fields. My grandfather was born in Germany so he could speak to them in their own language.
Ron Vannelli

Allied Help.
Manchester, 1940's.

Although we lived close to Manchester I was not evacuated. We kids carried gas masks with us all the time. I also wore something called a siren suit which was an all-in-one piece of clothing made of blanket material similar to a babygro. The suits were to help keep us warm when in the air raid shelter. There was rivalry in the shelter for the topmost bunk. I was always fighting with a couple of lads for it.

An American forces base was nearby and it is true to say we asked the Soldiers and Airmen for confectionery. "Have you got any gum, chum?" we'd say, and often we'd get a huge block of chocolate.
Polly Hackett

Coal, Gas Masks and Bombers.
Evacuee's Memories of Merthyr.

The school had coal fired heating. Coal was delivered monthly in Merthyr and had to last until the next delivery. If the coal ran out and the heating went off we would have to stand by our desks every half hour and jump up and down to keep warm. We carried gas masks with us everywhere. It wasn't that we were bothered too much about it though we knew that Cardiff and Swansea were being bombed but we saw nothing of it until one night a German bomber got lost and came down nearby. Everyone came out of their houses with the excitement of it. It felt like Christmas.

Pat Johnson (née Shine)

Salvage.

After I came home to Sidcup I remember the dugout in our front garden with grey blankets. At school we had a big campaign to collect salvage with rewards in terms of military ranks according to the amount collected. I was extremely proud to become a Major!

Anita Halliday

Evacuated.

When the war started our schooling was badly affected. We had to go in late some days due to heavy bombing during the night. I can't remember why but I know groups of us were taught in people's front rooms, possibly due to utilities being damaged. We lived in Main Street off the Stratford Road and we endured lots of air raids, the BSA Works being not far away. We had a lot of bomb damage. The top of our road was levelled one night by land mines and I lost two friends in air raids. During the war we were evacuated. My brother had just started school and I must have been almost nine years old. Needless to say it

Evacuees with gas masks, bags and labels during the Second World War.

was another upset. We were taken from school in coaches – charabancs – to the railway station. Parents didn't come to the station. Most of us were crying or in shock. Sandwiches and drinks were provided on the train. After our rail journey we boarded coaches again and were taken to a large school hall. I seemed to be miles away from home but we were in Ibstock, Leicestershire. We must have looked a sorry bunch, the lucky ones carrying little cases, others clutching carrier bags, and a gas mask hanging round our necks. People came to the hall and picked children to take into their homes. My brother and I must have looked unappealing because we were almost the last to be chosen by a lady who became a second mother to me.

Patricia Green (née Rowbotham)

All The Spuds You Can Eat.
Deykin Avenue School, Witton.
After the war my class was taken twice a week by chara – coach – to a local farm to pick potatoes. I can't remember how many weeks this went on. I don't think we were ever paid.
Ron Wilkinson

CHANGING TIMES

Another Year.
Clifton Road School, early 20th Century.
My two elder sisters left school at 13 years of age and they had just passed a law that I had to stop until 14 years. My mother thought it was awful that she had to keep me for months without me working and earning.
Annie Farrington, (née Bickerstaff)

Clearing Off In The Teachers' Strike.
It was 1985 and I went to George Dixon School. The Teachers' Strike was on and all the kids had decided that as the teachers were on strike they were going on strike too. So halfway through the morning there were more and more kids going out into the playground. They had locked the gates to keep us all in but my brother said "Follow me." We all went to the gates, climbed over and went home, so I finished my first day at one o'clock.
James Hobbs

Exams In The Teachers' Strike.
Ten weeks before the GCSE examinations there was a national strike by teachers. We were given work to take home. I didn't bother with it. There was no further support – that was it. We were left to revise at home. I did not do any revision, such was my interest. We sat the exams in portacabins brought in for the purpose, as the school hadn't the space to carry them out.
Marion Ridsdill

Winds of Change.
Turves Green.
Social, religious, and educational change was in the air during my last years at school. It was noticeable that some of the school pupils were not attending assemblies where Christian hymns were sung or prayers said. My queries on the matter ascertained that there were a number of children from Jehovah Witness

families. The ethnic changes to the population were being reflected by black and Asian faces among the new intakes. My final year at school, 1972, was the very last year that there was a choice of leaving education at 15 years old, or staying on to take CSE's. If you decided to leave, you were given a Leaving Certificate to say you had done OK at school. I left. I decided that I couldn't stop at school any longer. I still have my school leaving and tap-dancing certificates.
Sally Williams (née Hall)

Mods And Rockers.
There was plenty of parking space at or near the school, which provided the sight of many Vespa scooters lined up, as there were many 'Mods' – of Mods & Rockers styling – among pupils. They rode into school dressed in long capes and Doc Martin boots. This was possible because school uniform was not compulsory during the final student year.
Patsy Stewart

Exams And Tests.
Perry Beeches, 1986/7.
I came to the time of exams and tests in the middle of the Thatcher years. It was 1985–6 and the teaching professions were not happy with their lot, taking strike action. It was also a time of change in the education world. O levels were being phased out and GCSE's phased in. Help from teachers was not the best at a time when we needed it most, gearing up for exams. After preparing for O level Maths for some time, suddenly I was given a choice between taking the CSE or O level exam. I chose CSE but it was the wrong choice. I was not happy with the results as I did not get the grade I wanted.

I didn't have any problem leaving school. I remember the Careers Advisors who were a product of their time. They had been trained, (or, is that tainted?) with the Youth Training Scheme syndrome of careers advice. It amounted to virtually one theme. It didn't seem to matter what the individual wanted, "I would like to take up a place in a tech college, doing graphics." "Have you thought about a YTS placement?"... "I'd like to go into further education." "Have you thought about a YTS placement?"... I managed to get a place at Matthew Boulton Tech to further my education.
Peter Cole

Chapter 6

Leaving

More memorable times! For some, leaving school was the dreaded end of everything good and a sense of loss and regret springs out. For some there was apprehension over an uncertain future whether it was to be work or marriage. Surprisingly, in view of the many negative memories earlier, no one claims to have been overjoyed to leave.

Leaving For Australia.
1955.
My first memory of infant school was the day I left!

I was five and a half years old and I think the reason I remember the day so well is because my teacher had taken my hand and led me to the Headmaster's office. I knew I wasn't in trouble because she was smiling at me, but I had no idea why she was being so nice. The Headmaster also smiled and talked at me. I think it was something about going on a big ship, and he gave me the gift of a book. He looked very pleased but I can vividly remember that I wasn't and remember asking for a doll instead! My teacher wasn't smiling on the walk back to class.

Janet Jones (née Blewitt)

Entertaining Teacher.
Budapest, 1980's.
When it comes to leaving primary school it is treated as a big occasion in Hungary. It's a special celebration time. We kids dressed up beautifully and went to the hairdressers and wore make-up, which was allowed. We were bought presents and flowers and given money by our parents and other relations, some travelling a long way to come and see us. One school class at a time would go to visit their teacher in his or her home. Most of us were armed with musical instruments. We would sing and play music outside, hopefully good enough – it was always good enough – to be invited into the teacher's house or flat where we would drink with them and play and sing again.

Laura Szendy

Dance, Laugh, Cry.
Meadows Primary.
We always had end of year parties but this one was more poignant. Everyone in their best clothes and for the first time I remember us dancing to music on a portable record player, songs by T. Rex, Slade, Sweet, The Osmonds etc. The last song played was Crocodile Rock by Elton John. Then we all left and there were a few, all girls, in tears as we said goodbye. I think most of us went back to visit once or twice after we started our new schools but it all seemed different and you realised you had moved on literally and in spirit – so we didn't go back again.
Chris Sutton

School Days Are The Best.
We did our exams and then we went back to school to finish the term out. We would bring in games and just mess about.

I remember when I was younger the older kids who were leaving would throw egg and flour, cut up their blazers and throw their bras onto the fields. School days are the best days but you just don't realise it then!
Pam Mullin

Jobs For The Plebs.
1950's.
As I grew older I became aware that there was a service at the school for leavers, and that it took the same form every year, with the same hymns and prayers. Then suddenly one day the service is for you, it's your turn to leave.

A couple of weeks or so before leaving school for good we were asked, with regard to employment, what we would like to be. There were a number of choices for us plebs; electrician, plumber, milkman etc, etc. The silly thing was that at that time we were likely to get our choice, there were that many jobs around.
Dennis Hammond

Job Preparation.
I left school at the age of 15 years. The school or local government body arranged for us school leavers to visit some of the larger local firms such as Cadburys and Dunlop, to give us an idea of the work environment and help us to decide what we might like to do in terms of a job. My mother paid for shorthand and typing lessons, and this led to my first job in an office in the city centre.
Pat Johnson (née Shine)

Tears For The Clown.
Smethwick Hall Girls Secondary School, 1967.
I was given a flower arranging book by Miss Marshall during the end of term assembly, and we all had one of those autograph books that everybody signed with comments. People wrote that they would always remember me as the 'clown' or for the fact of my appearances in the school plays. We sang "Jerusalem" and as I looked around everybody was crying.
Marcia Vizor

Farewell Music.
Wallasey High School, 1960's.
Strangely I have little memory of my last school day, except for the final assembly and the realisation that I would never again stand on that balcony looking down on the rest of the school, singing hymns to the distinguished and much-loved music master's piano accompaniment. The days of wild cavorting and signing of shirts on the last day, so enjoyed by leavers today, had not yet arrived.
Wendy Beynon (née Forsyth)

Moving On.
My last few days of school were busy and emotional I didn't really want to leave as I had become comfortable. I remember saying good-bye, signing tee-shirts and things like that and then in the evening my friends and me went for meals. There was this one girl who got pregnant halfway through the year, which I think was hard for her, and another girl in my class was pregnant whilst she was sitting her exams.
Sadia Majid

Looking Back.
Towards the end of school there was a mixture of confusion and apprehension about the future. I know some of the girls were nervous because they knew they had to go abroad to get married. I wasn't sure whether I could cope with college but my friends encouraged me and I went to college. I still have my shirt and autograph book from school. I think if I went back now I'd concentrate more and make different friends.
Dalal Olewa

In The Book.
Rushcliffe, Nottingham, 1990's.
I did well in my studies and exams and got 10 GCSE's. For the leaving party we wore our white blouses and brought marker pens to write messages on them. 'I will miss you', 'I love you' and even 'I hate you' – in a fun way. The school also

organised a Leaving Year Book where all the leavers were listed by name and birthday details. For some reason I never got my copy. However I still keep in touch with a lot of my school mates by way of Facebook.
Selina Brown

Senior Year Presentation.
Wyoming Country Schooling.
It was the final or senior year before Thermopolis would put on a celebration of its pupils' achievements. Those of us who were leaving would gather together at a formal presentation. The number one person who had the top marks overall would get to deliver the graduation speech 'Valedictorian'. This was usually a girl. A guest speaker would also entertain the assembly. This could be a local celebrity or a past pupil made good in the outside world. The school's 'T' motif would be everywhere and cheerleaders would be present. The annual yearbook carrying a picture of every final year school kid would be on display with captions such as, 'The most popular student', 'The best looking girl' or 'The best looking boy'.
Ron Vannelli

The Last Day.
Graduation from High School is a big deal in America; there is a lot of ceremony attached to it. An assembly takes place where you have to go up to the front and receive your graduation certificate. We also had graduation rings to wear, and of course there was the 'Prom'.
Samantha Hines

Speech Day.
Chelmsford High School held a Speech day each year to award prizes and Exam Certificates for those who had left. By chance, the year I left was a special one and so I found that my awards were being presented by the Queen Mother.
Val Hart (née Cooper)

It's The End.
My last days of school were quite funny and we had a good laugh.

Speech Day for Chelmsford High School, Essex. Val Hart (née Cooper) receives prizes from the Queen Mother. 1959.

I think everybody was under the realisation that it was all coming to an end and that they would eventually start moving away from each other. I think that brought every one together.

Jahan Mahmood

Final Get-Together.
Kenya, 1998.

My best day at school was the last day. We had gone on a trip to see the traditional African way of living. I never saw some of those kids again so it was nice to have a last day like that with them.

Sukaina Khimji

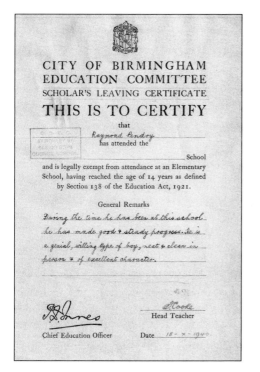 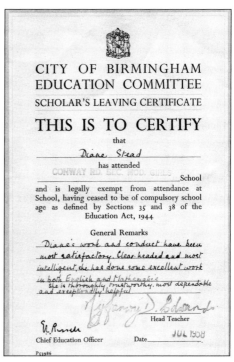

Left: Leaving Certificate for Raymond Pendry, 1940. Right: Leaving Certificate for Diane Stead. Conway Rd Secondary Modern School, Sparkbrook, Birmingham. 1958.

In Conclusion

Balsall Heath Local History Society would like to thank all those who have contributed memories, documents and photographs to this book. It was not possible to include everything that was recorded but it will all be retained in the Society Archives as a valuable and unique collection of source material.

Exam Certificate, 1888.

List of Interviewees

Nowrah Abdul

Abdulahi Ahmed

Sabreena Ali

Joyce Ashworth

Shahida Aslam

Jim Atkinson

Len Baron

John Bealt

Rakhiya Begum

Winifred Berkeley

Wendy Beynon (née Forsyth)

Shashi Bhana

Nazreen Bi

Sameera Bi

Zainab Bi

Sayma Bibi

Jack Billington

John William Brown

Reginald Arthur Brown

Selina Brown

Tesh Champaneri

Maurice Cleaver

Peter Cole

Peter Davis

Bob Dearing

Marion Dimulias (née Brown)

Tracy Doherty

Helen Donaghy

Olive Dowdeswell (née Rose)

Pamela Douglas (née Blenkiron)

Albert Eaton

Maurice Arthur Evans

Annie Farrington (née Bickerstaff)

Michael Henry Fitzpatrick

Ron Ford

Gladys Ford (née Woolley)

Valerie Ganderton

Bob Greenway

Patricia Green

Stephen Gwynne

Anjum Gul

Polly Hackett

Anita Halliday

Dennis Hammond

Jack Harris

Valerie Harris (née Farrant)

Val Hart (née Cooper)

Alan Hemming

Anne Hemming

Ann Hill (née Graham)

O.G. Hill (Mrs)

Samantha Hines

James Hobbs

Scott Hosker

Mark Houldcroft

Ron Hubbell

Bernard Jackson

Rizwan Janmohamed

Victoria Jeffs

Yvette John

Pat Johnson (née Shine)

Emily Jones (née Belcher)

Janet Jones

Ishtiaq Khan

Sheikh Amina Khanum

Razia Khatun

Sukaina Khimji

Jo Lea

Jahan Mahmood
Sadia Majid
Dawn McGhie
Neil Monroe
Pam Mullin
Dalal Olewa
Mrs Osborne
Peter Owusu
Graham Pearson
Rose Pearson
Len Powell
Alan Price
Barbara Rainbird
Abdullah Rehman
Sheila Reynolds (née Moore)
Marion Ridsdill
Yvonne Rollins (née Stead)
Neelam Rose
Bron Salway
Pete Salway
Nisha Sharma
Deborah Simpson (née Style)
Kerry Smith
Maureen Smith

Naseem Somani
Naveed Somani
Russell Spring
Diane Stead
Patsy Stewart
Ally Sultana
Chris Sutton
Steve Sutton
Laura Szendy
Errol Thomas
Betty Thornicroft
Ann Tolbutt
Ron Vannelli
Marcia Vizor
Iram Weir
Gwen White
Nell Wilkins
Marie Wilkinson (née Collins)
Ron Wilkinson
Sally Williams (née Hall)
Carol Woolley
Ted Wright
Sohail Yousef

Named Schools

Adams Hill, Bartley Green, Birmingham

Aga Khan Foundation. Pakistan

Albert Bradbeer Primary School, Longbridge, Birmingham

Audley Road Secondary School, Stechford, Birmingham

Belgrave School, (formerly Mary Street School) Balsall Heath, Birmingham

Bishop Challoner RC School, Kings Heath, Birmingham

Blue Coat School, Birmingham

British Catholic School, Madhya Pradesh. India

Brooklyn State School, Melbourne. Australia

Bygate Infant School, Whitley Bay, Northumberland

Castlepollard Parochial School, County Westmeath. Ireland

Chelmsford County High School for Girls, Essex

Chislehurst and Sidcup Grammar School for Girls, Kent

Christchurch C of E School, Sparkbrook, Birmingham

Clifton Road, Balsall Heath, Birmingham

College Road, Springfield, Birmingham

Colmer's Farm School, Birmingham

Conway Secondary School, Sparkbrook, Birmingham

Dennis Road School, (later renamed Anderton Park School) Sparkhill, Birmingham

Deykin Avenue School, Witton, Birmingham

Dudley Road Council School, Birmingham

Embassy School, Pretoria. South Africa

Evander Child High School, New York. USA

Francis Road School, Bournville, Birmingham

Friars School, Bangor. North Wales

George Betts C of E, Handsworth, Birmingham

George Dixon, Edgbaston, Birmingham

Glebe Farm Park, Birmingham

Glendo School, Wyoming. USA

Grove Park Grammar School for Girls, Wrexham

Heath Mount Junior and Infant School, Balsall Heath, Birmingham

Jaffray Academy, Mombassa. Kenya

Jakeman Road Nursery School, Balsall Heath, Birmingham

Kewdale High School. Australia
King Edward's Grammar School, Camp Hill, Birmingham
Kings Heath Technical School, Birmingham
Kings Norton Grammar School, Birmingham
Ladywood Follett School, Ladywood, Birmingham
Langley Avenue CP School, Whitley Bay, Northumberland
Lawfield's Primary School, Wakefield
Loxton Street Junior School, Nechells, Birmingham
Manderson School, Wyoming. USA
Mary Street School, (later renamed Belgrave School) Balsall Heath, Birmingham
Meadows School, Northfield, Birmingham
Merrywood Grammar School for Girls, Bristol
Merthyr RC School. Wales
Mico Practising School. Jamaica. West Indies
Moseley C of E National School, Moseley, Birmingham
Moseley School of Art, Balsall Heath, Birmingham
Mount Pleasant Secondary School, Balsall Heath, Birmingham
New Broughton Primary School, Wrexham
Open Air School, Birmingham
Perry Beeches School, Birmingham
Rea Street School, Highgate, Birmingham
Rushcliffe Secondary School, Nottingham
Sandy Point Primary School, St Kitts. West Indies
Sherbourne Road School, Balsall Heath, Birmingham
Sidcup Hill School, Kent
Smethwick Hall Girls Secondary School, Smethwick
South Bunbury Primary School. Australia
Springfield Junior and Infant School, Birmingham
St Alban's School, Highgate, Birmingham
St Anne's School, Chelmsford, Essex
St Clement's Junior School, Nechells, Birmingham
St David's School, Rea Street, Birmingham
St George's Primary School, Wallasey, Cheshire
St John's RC School, Balsall Heath, Birmingham
St Luke's School, Birmingham
St Thomas C of E, Ladywood, Birmingham
Steward Street School, Ladywood, Birmingham
Sunyani Boarding School, Broig Ahato Region. Ghana
Thermopolis High School, Wyoming. USA

Tindal Street School, Balsall Heath, Birmingham
Tudor Grange School, Solihull, Birmingham
Turves Green Girls School, Turves Green, Birmingham
Uplands Secondary Modern School, Smethwick
Upper Highgate School, Birmingham
Victoria School, Northfield, Birmingham
Vizafogo Primary School, Angyalfold. Budapest
Wakefield High School for Girls, Wakefield
Wallasey High School, Wallasey, Cheshire
Waverley Grammar School for Girls, Small Heath, Birmingham
Wheelers Lane, Kings Heath, Birmingham
Woodfall School, Neston, Cheshire
Woodview School, Edgbaston, Birmingham
Wythall Village School
Ysgol y Gadr. Wales

Key Changes to the English Education System in the 20th Century

1. 1902. The Balfour Act
This empowered Local Authorities to provide secondary education.

2. 1918. The Fisher Act
The school leaving age was raised to 14.

3. 1944. The Butler Act
This aimed to provide a secondary education for all in accordance with "age, ability and aptitude" and set up the tripartite system of Grammar, Secondary Modern and Technical Schools. Access to Grammar Schools was by means of a selection test which was popularly called the 11+. The Act also required all state aided schools to provide collective religious worship daily.

4. 1947.
The school leaving age was raised to 15.

5. 1964 onwards
Although no legislation was passed by the new Labour Government, Local Authorities were encouraged to move towards a system of Comprehensive (non-selective) schools.

6. 1972.
The school leaving age was raised to 16.

7. 1988. The Education Reform Act
This established the National Curriculum and set up the system of League Tables so that schools' achievements could be compared.

Index of People and Places